Creating a New Version of You

Sheryl L. Brown, LMFT

Opulence Publishing

Opulence
PUBLISHING

Cumming, Georgia

Role Model Production. Inc.: Opulence Publishing
Cumming, GA 30041

ISBN Paperback 978-0-9896254-2-5

Printed in the United States of America

Library of Congress Control Number: 2022913638

Endorsements

I have to be honest with you. From the time I started reading this book, I absolutely could not put the book down. It was as if I was sitting in front of Sheryl as she spoke these words. All throughout the book, I was thinking I needed this book years ago. As I read each chapter there were gentle nudges letting me know there was still residue of pain in certain areas. I thought surely, I had gotten over it but sometimes pain comes in layers that you must work through and not around. I immediately started implementing Sheryl's advice on how to truly forgive. As Sheryl touched on the various topics, I could see my past and current life unfold within each chapter. Reading the excerpt on being on Autopilot resonated with me because that was me. Years ago, I was going through life being a busybody, but I was not being productive. I was wearing too many hats and these hats were not mine. Hmmm…interesting. Did you hear me? Some were not mine. Have you ever sat and brood over why you were doing something that was not enhancing your life? So, why was I doing this? It was not enhancing me, but it provided me a way of escaping my reality. I had curved over into someone else's lane. I was wearing a hat with the name wife on it, but he was not my husband. What I mean by that is he was not the man God intended for me to be married to. I had to learn that one plus one does not equal three. I had to look at the situation as it was and stop pretending it was something else.

In my previous marriage, I was so busy caring for my children, the house, and trying to balance the stress of a toxic marriage. I lost myself. Somewhere in the mix was me and I had no clue who I was, what I wanted or needed. I was drained. Burnt out on the ups and downs of a fantasized marriage I created. Did you catch that? I created it. See rushing into things and allowing outside pressure to make your decisions creates unwanted chaos and heartache. I had to say goodbye to chaos and heartache. I could no longer allow the two to become a mortgage in my life. When you jump ahead of God's plan there is no peace.

During my previous marriage, I did not know the benefits of mastering the art of saying no. Sheryl states that "constantly saying yes can oftentimes interfere with the timing in which the individual should actually experience or receive the tangible manifestation in his or her life." I knew that marriage was not a manifestation from God, but I was more concerned about the money that had been spent instead of calling off the wedding. Everything about it was all wrong. The timing, the person, and reasons for getting married. Hear me when I say this. I mean this in love. He was not the one for me and I was not the one for him. You may wonder if I am still working on becoming a better me. Yes, I am. I purposely read the chapters twice to digest the information in order to apply it to my life. One thing that is helping me master the art of saying no today is setting clear boundaries with others. Setting boundaries helps me to protect my mind and peace.

Sheryl spoke about "entering into the wrong circles." I cannot say this enough. I wish I had this book years ago. It would have saved time invested in circles I never belonged in. Sheryl also mentioned that "everyone is not your friend." This was a hard pill to swallow. It took me many years to recognize this because I am fun, friendly and I like to see others shine. My kindness often led others to believe I would accept light switch friendships. One day they want to be your friend and the next week they switch up. I used to ask God if I did something wrong or say something that was not kind.

Once I recognized this was a pattern and/or recurrent behavior, I stopped asking myself if I did something wrong. I stopped questioning why and when people walked out of my life. Now, I purposely stay away from light switch friendships. However, I accept the fact that seasonal friendships come with an expiration date. Also, it is okay to outgrow people. Before I enter into any friendships, I now ask myself how this friendship would benefit my emotional well-being. The book took me to a deeper thought process of why it is important for me to know "when it's time to exit a circle." One thing I realized about myself while reading this book is my attachment style. When I meet quality people, I like to keep them around. What I have come to realize is everyone does not want that same attachment.

Since reading this book and gaining more insight. I am careful about my time, the people I allow around me, conversations, my self-care, and my PEACE. Today, I am taking Sheryl's advice by making sure I take breaks. Breaks from people, work and social media. This allows me quiet time with God. It centers me, it gives me peace and I make better decisions. I am adamant about removing all toxicity out of my life. I am ready to wear my hats as Sheryl says "authentically, effectively, and confidently." Sheryl, thank you for being obedient. This book has a wealth of nuggets. I plan to use this book to help the women I service. You truly have a gift of writing, healing, and restoring life. If you are reading my testimony, I encourage you to read this book, read it again, digest every word and apply it to create a NEW VERSION OF YOU.

–Pamela Shakir,
Licensed Clinical Social Worker
Author of *Creative Strategies: A Self-Guided Journal To Help You Kick Depression*

Endorsements

The charge Sheryl Brown has taken on with the subject of finding your authenticity, revelation, and celebration of self in this wonderful project, is truly uplifting, beyond what my words can convey.

"Bravo" Sheryl, for opening Pandora's box of our "ments", that is truly crippling our society!!! Entitlement, resentment, abandonment of your value and worth, etc. The troubling notion to please the masses, is putting many in very isolated and threatening situations, where our social media is trying to gloss over this and similar concerns as "daily news."

Thank you for challenging the reader, who will welcome this book with the areas in your chapters that includes, thought-provoking questions, daily challenges for improvement; establishing real boundaries, keeping your dreams and passions sacred. You are giving the reader the true reminders and techniques of projecting an image of confidence, versus doubt, where you give guidance to really reinvent yourself; to get back to your true and satisfying joy. Every chapter has left me with writing notes to myself to reflect upon, as well as engage with women, especially, our younger women; seeking the mentorship and guidance of a spirit and motivation to guide them in the right path of success. Clearly, a text that can lend itself in and out of many circles of individuals, who are soul searching and seeking the motivation, to carry on in their immediate concerns, to the celebrations to make sure your life is well lived.

This "project for the soul", is riveting, rejuvenating, and refreshing, for your depth of being candid, honest, and bold, with the revelations we need to inventory within ourselves... I think many of us need to read in black and white to really get to the just of our "true existence". You have peeled back many layers, we have tried to hide for too long and now again, as a society, the suffrage is real, and the mental and spiritual healing is at an all-time high. I certainly chart this wonderful project on the bestsellers list for motivation and self-help with "5 Stars"!!!

Sheryl, I have always and will continue to applaud your gifts of "raising a crowd on their feet", to now, "getting us to read\ sit down" for a few hours with this incredible book and "find yourself", "celebrate yourself", and "treasure yourself" to the fullest.

Thank you, Sheryl for bringing a true "page turner", for the summer, that is guaranteed to feed the masses with hope and joy of being your best self.

Andrea Caldwell
Director/Mentor
Stepping Stones Youth Development Program

Dedication

This book is dedicated to all the women who have endlessly sacrificed the authenticity of self for the sake of depositing into the lives of those who are connected to the many hats you wear in life.

For those of you who have suppressed the hurt, betrayal, shame, guilt, rejection, abandonment, and abuse, as a result of being on active duty to serve, love, impart, guide, nurture, and resolve, I salute you. It is your time, your season to create and embrace the new version of yourself.

To my husband for being part of my destiny. Thank you for being my best friend, my companion, and my soul mate.

To our little Princess Paris, you have brought so much joy into our lives. Thank you for giving mommy the seal of approval on the artwork for this book.

To my parents, Shellie and Christine Stewart who taught me the importance of acknowledging God in all my ways.

To family and friends whose life experiences are gently embedded within the content of this book. Thank you for listening, sharing, imparting wisdom, and most importantly praying during the process of writing *Many Hats*. And special thanks to Gwendolyn Stone for her unwaivering committment in helping bring to this book to fruition. Love you Stoneth.

God, I thank you for giving me the Grace to do what I was assigned to even during the midst of opposition. I completely depend on you.

Let the Journey begin.
The New Version of you awaits.

Contents

Forward

During this journey called life, we are faced with a plethora of decisions. Life takes on a different pace at different seasons. Life can change course and pace at a moment's notice without your permission. Many are confronted with choices, challenges, and changes. You ask yourself, "What now?" Why is it always something? Just when you are finally at a place of rest, a place of progress, a place of triumph, there is something else that challenges you to pause. You pause at least for a moment to gather yourself. You gather all the emotions from life's instant and surprising interruptions. Life can make you feel like you are playing dress-up. Sometimes you feel like you can conquer the world, and at other times you may feel defeated and beat down. No matter what the choices, challenges, or changes are, know that you are not all by yourself even though it may appear you are. May God's peace and His amazing grace give you the fortitude to relax, welcome peace, withstand fear and the confidence in knowing that you are well able of being strong while taking on life's trials as you wear many hats. You are equipped with a finishing grace to complete each task, even when thoughts of defeat are trying to overthrow and conquer you during the times when you are already winning.

How do we as women, men included, pursue greatness, education, family life, entrepreneurship, the ideal mate, the dream job, etc., when we are constantly faced with life and the responsibility that life brings every day? How can you pursue the very thing in your heart that you desire so passionately when there is so much to do? How do you do it all? How do you even pursue it without becoming burnt out? How does one keep their pursuits in contrast and remain content without running on empty? How do we release the insecurity, shame, guilt, feelings of rejection, hurt, etc., so that we can properly impart meaning into the lives of those who withdraw from the many hats we wear? This timely book, *Many Hats: Creating A New Version of You*, will strategically teach you how to maintain the authenticity of self while navigating through this journey called life.

This beautifully written book will assist you to explore the depths of your thought processes when emotions are raging and the fight of life is loud when continuous scenarios of life are approaching. And do not forget that someone is waiting on you to impart into them so they can live a greater, victorious life. At moments, it is difficult to lead when life is leaning on your shoulders. Here is the kicker, the call on your life will not let you stop; despite the test, the passion within pushes you to keep going. We are expected to show up for others before we show up for ourselves. We are expected to perform. So, you must work to become a better you while life reminds you of your responsibilities. Sheryl Brown passionately gives us descriptions and principles to stand by in life that will help you create balance for you to live healthily and prosperously. She has created simple daily routines and activities for you to glean from. Her strategy is for you to look deeper and benefit from her words. I love how she gave examples of how we can become lost and exhausted by operating on autopilot! That is a NO! Thank you, Sheryl, for reminding us to refuel before we run out of gas. Unhealthy! You've got to love yourself before you pour into others: "You cannot pour from an empty cup." You will read about this issue in this insightful book of awareness of self.

A gift that you can give to yourself is applying what has been written in these pages to your life and making the adjustments that will enable you to have a promising future with boundaries that will remind you how important you are to yourself. I would like to challenge you to dig, dive deeper, and demand your heart to be opened to receive. Start your journey through this text with the deep self-reflection written by Sheryl Brown: "Remember your ability to wear your hat or hats effectively is based on how you think." You will now enter into becoming a masterpiece by reading these pages. I invite you to begin creating a new version of yourself so that you can wear your many hats gracefully and confidently.

–Vicki L. Kemp
Bestselling author of
Better Than Yesterday & *Grace in Deep Waters*

Preface

Have you noticed how time is accelerating like never before? One moment we are bringing in the New Year with our "good intentions" and resolutions. The next moment, we are celebrating Thanksgiving with family and friends, embracing and sharing the love, laughter, and reasons for being thankful, all while we are gratifying our palates with scrumptious food that accentuates the holiday spirits.

As we live in sync with the progression of time, better known as life, the responsibilities and commitments attached to our family life, career, community, church, etc. are constantly tugging from our innate ability to serve. Let the truth be told, our plates are always full and rarely empty as we endlessly search for more time to complete the task at hand. Amazingly enough, regardless of the size of our plates or the amount of time designated to complete our assignments, we have mastered the skill of multitasking. Why? During the course of multitasking, you and I have unconsciously created an assortment of customized hats that we wear interchangeably everyday while we occupy in the capacity of mother, wife, grandmother, aunt, daughter, friend, career woman, college student, mentor, entrepreneur and on and on. Wearing many hats ultimately becomes part of our identity, but each as a separate entity. In other words, one person, but many hats or roles. This swapping is quite helpful from the standpoint that it allows you and me to effectively separate each role we play in the lives of others so that we can properly attend to their needs in a proper fashion. These hats are made from durable fabrics, such as wisdom, patience, nurturing, encouragement, caring, dependability, and protection, all of which are held together by the thread which I call love.

However, this innate gift, multitasking, that has been so graciously bestowed on us as women, is constantly on the "ON" mode and very rarely on the "OFF" mode. In other words, we are fulfilling daily commitments if we feel like it or not. We take our children to school, soccer practice, etc., if we feel like it or not. We cook dinner for our family after a long, hard day at work if we feel like it or not. We get up early in the morning to go to work if we feel like it or not. We take time to lend a listening hear to someone who is hurting when we are hurting ourselves. Over the course of time, we find ourselves giving of self, sacrificing self no matter how we feel, or what we are going through (the challenges we face). Let the truth be told, our emotional, mental, and physical gauge is running on empty as we attend to the needs of those who are connected one way or another to the many hats we wear. There are women right now from all walks of life who are at their posts diligently serving, imparting into the lives of others, but at the same time walking around silently depressed. One issue away from breaking down, these women are overwhelmed and even frustrated as a result of being emotionally, physically, and mentally drained because of the excessive withdrawals made from those around them and not enough deposits made in between or in return.

Like never before, I feel an urgency to write this book for those women, including you, who have lost the essence of "Self" along the way and are desperately in need of a new version of YOU. There are those of us at one time or another who have worn hats that either have lost their shape - crooked, faded in color, and loose at the seam. We often find ourselves walking around in a daze, like robots fulfilling predesigned roles, but not feeling complete due to forfeiting our right to a balanced life.

Ladies, if it is expected for us to wear many hats, then we need to know how to wear our hats correctly. A woman who wears her hat with style and confidence is a woman who has learned the importance of living a balanced life. She understands the importance of depositing back into self so that there will be a sufficient amount of "Self" to withdraw from. As you read *Many Hats*, my desire is that you will give yourself permission to take care of you. Validating your purpose here on this earth first starts with you taking care of you. Therefore, by consistently employing the principles and recommendations introduced to you through the various chapters of this book, you will gain insight, strength, confidence, rejuvenation, inner healing, and peace that results from not only living a balanced life but knowing how to operate effectively in your vein. Enjoy your journey as you create a new version of you so that you can wear your *Many Hats* with style and purpose.

Sincerely,
Sheryl L. Brown

Chapter 1

SELF, LOST IN THE MIX

One of my personal outlets in life that allows me to stay in touch with myself is working out at the gym. I like to go early in the morning before the sun rises and right before the birds greet the new day with a harmonious, naturistic melody. While working out at the gym, I try to keep my conversations at a minimum so that I can get the most out of my workout. However, there are times, more often than not, that I engage in a brief conversation with someone while lifting weights or jogging on the treadmill. One morning while I was driving to the gym, I was on day two of pondering whether or not it was time to write this book you are currently reading. I have found when the content within the book is seasoned, when it's ripe, there is much to be gained for those who will properly digest and apply the information provided in their lives accordingly.

As I completed my workout and was about to head downstairs to exit the center, I ran into one of my beautiful gym associates that I casually converse with throughout the week. Normally, she and I would compliment each other on the progress we observe during our body transformation journey. Each time I had the opportunity to be in her presence, she always greeted me with a big, genuine smile. However, this particular day there something notably different about my friend. Her body language appeared to be expressing that she was disgruntled, dissatisfied, and exhausted, but at the same time she was making every effort to mask what seemed obvious with her radiant smile. As we were talking, I asked her if everything was okay. She replied with tears welling up in her eyes, "I am not happy! I feel like I have lost myself in all that I do! I have become everything to everybody that I do not even know who I am anymore." Wow! How many of you have ever felt like self was lost in the mix at some point in your life? At that moment, I had my answer; it was definitely time to write this book. I have learned to never take for granted the encounters we have with others, for there could possibly be an answer or confirmation awaiting you through the exchange of words.

On Autopilot

I have come to the conclusion that we have grown accustomed to our lives being set on autopilot. As we strategically rearrange our schedules to make sure the daily routines, obligations, and/or events attached to the hat or hats we wear are promptly attended to, we fail to etch out some time to land in order to refuel our bodies, minds, and emotions for the journey ahead. Furthermore, we have helplessly submitted to the self-created excuses that have become the hallmarks we use to validate the reason or reasons for being hesitant when it comes to reuniting with self. Just because we have unconsciously equated operating from an autopilot mode as being normal does not make it right. When we are constantly on autopilot and deny ourselves the opportunity to take the time to attend to self, we cause our emotions and thoughts to be at odds with each other and out of sync, therefore giving rise to mental and physical fatigue, emotional instability, and even becoming susceptible to various ailments.

This combative struggle to maintain soundness of mind, physical health, and emotional stability in order to preserve the authenticity of self is often negated by the constant surrendering of oneself. You constantly deny self for the sake of those who are endless-ly pulling from the unconditional love, wisdom, faith, patience, strength, determination, leadership abilities, discernment, disci-pline, emotional support, nurturing qualities, and creativity that has been proportionally distributed in each hat you wear. It is when we, as women, fail to find a balance between all that is required from the hat or hats worn and taking time to care for self, that we find ourselves lost in the mix. As a result, we become burned out, depressed, stressed, frustrated, bitter, moody, or on the edge, causing our hats to tilt to one side when they should be standing straight up on top of our heads.

My friend at the gym was experiencing a mental overload due to her identity being constantly pushed in the background as she sacrificed self for others. I must admit there is not only a sense of honor but also an indescribable sense of gratification when serving others. But at the same time, there can be what I call an unsettledness within as a result of self being lost in the mix, causing the drive to reunite with self to be at a minimum. For that reason, the sense of pleasure becomes numb because the mind is exhausted. I have found where there is no sense of pleasure, there is no strength. Where there is no strength, there is no desire; and where there is no desire, there is a dissatisfaction with self. Where there is a dissatisfaction with self, there is no passion. And where there is no passion, it becomes a chore to remain fully focused and committed towards the purpose behind the hat or hats worn. The talents, gifts, decisions, dependency, enthusiasm, and/or service to others are not at its highest performance as when you are mentally alert.

I can recall a time in my life when my identity of self was being camouflaged by the high level of demands being placed on my life. Whether it was because of extensive traveling with my husband, fulfilling our pre-scheduled speaking engagements, or coming home to serve as a wife, mother, or cleaning lady, something on the inside did not feel at ease. I was becoming vulnerable to an unwarranted unsettledness within, which was holding my thoughts and emotions captive. This seemingly unbeatable, unshakeable, and uncomfortable experience was robbing me of the unexplainable gratification I found in helping others, therefore causing me to feel like I was just existing rather than living. Have you ever felt like this? That is why it is crucial to periodically execute mental breaks so that the mind has time to rest and recharge itself. In chapter 2, I will go further in detail about the importance of reprogramming the mind and provide helpful techniques/exercises that will foster a healthy thought process.

Preventive Measures to Find Self

So, with all that has been said thus far, what preventive measures can we incorporate in our arsenal to preserve self in order to avoid becoming susceptible to the symptoms/signs associated with self being lost in the mix?

Preventive Measure # 1: Setting boundaries

Recovering and maintaining self from being lost in the mix weighs heavily on establishing boundaries that clearly differentiate between when it is time to serve others and when it is time to attend to self. For many, there are no lucid boundaries in place to undergird their personal life, causing the awareness of one's uniqueness, one's authenticity of self to become dim while the needs and/or the concerns of others become more heightened and vivid. Many women become prone to experience what I call a "burnt-out moment." A burnt-out moment is when an individual has over-exerted self to the point that she becomes no good to anyone, not even herself. Ladies (and gentlemen included), it is mandatory for boundaries to be strategically set in place in our lives: boundaries place a demand or set a standard in which not only you but those around you must respect your personal space. Let's be real, life is always about DOING. Cleaning up the house, taking your children to football practice, dance lessons, taking the dog to the groomer, going to the PTA meetings, fulfilling your duties as a wife, and overseeing a business meeting all fall under the category of DOING. Having your personal space is crucial from the standpoint that it allows you to enter into a place of rest, a "chill mode," where the opportunity is at hand for you to seize the moments to relax and regroup before resuming your designated roles. I highly recommend that all women should make it a habit to indulge in what I call a "bubble moment" on a regular basis. A bubble moment is when you become emotionally, mentally, and physically encapsulated in activities that not only bring you pleasure, but also usher in the serenity needed to tame one's emotions, physical health, and thoughts, such as jogging, reading a book while taking a warm relaxing bubble bath, hiking, etc. Me time, a bubble moment, literally becomes a spa treatment which permits you to pamper yourself in an effort to preserve the authenticity of self.

Establishing clear and solid boundaries help reshape people's per-spective (both personally and professionally) to not always see you as the solution. In addition, setting boundaries challenges you to avoid the temptations of being put in the position of constantly pro-viding the answer, offering yourself to execute the solution or both. For example, there is a high probability that the oldest sibling was introduced to various hats as early as childhood. Especially in the areas of attending to the needs of his or her younger siblings and/or raising them altogether. As a result, the roles and responsibilities connected to the hats created during childhood often are carried over into adulthood, enabling the younger "adult" siblings to automati-cally perceive (look upon) the oldest as being the go-to, the answer, when it comes to resolving family matters. By setting limits on how much you are willing to give of self, you will gradually force those around you to look outside of you in an effort to utilize or take ad-vantage of other accessible resources.

Preventive Measure #2: Mastering the Art of Saying NO

I hope you are cognizant of the fact that saying no is not a bad thing. Nor should saying no bring forth a strong sense of guilt, but rather an honest recognition that there may be times when you are unable or even unwilling to inconvenience yourself for the sake of meeting the needs of others. I hope that I am not presenting myself as having a callous regard for others, but people will always try to tap into your innate ability to resolve and/or make things happen. By you constantly saying yes and rarely saying no, you can possibly cause the following: 1) interference with an individual's opportunity of becoming more independent and less interdependent; and 2) impeding the timing of an individual's tangible manifestation in his or her life. For example, parents who endlessly say yes to their child, especially a child who is immature and irresponsible, can in many cases thwart his or her ability to grow and develop in the areas of patience. In addition, endless yesses prematurely expose the child to things and/or events that he or she may not be mentally or physically prepared to handle or appreciate. Constant yesses can also cause 3) inner resentment that begins to paint pictures on the canvas of your imagination, causing frustration, anxiety, and annoyance towards the person (or group) you are serving; and 4) disappointment with self for always saying yes when you really want to say no.

So, Sheryl, if I find it difficult to say no, what are some steps I can take toward saying no?

1. **Change your perception regarding the word no. No is not a bad word. See no as a decision and not a punishment.**

2. **Start saying no to the small things before saying no to the bigger things.**

3. **Do not be quick to respond. Analyze the request being made first and determine the following: 1) Does the request discredit your character in addition to what you believe? 2) Will it put me in harm's way and/or the person waiting on your response? 3) Why am I saying yes ? Is it because I do not want to be rejected, but rather accepted? and 4) Will all parties involved (including me benefit from me saying yes?**

4. **Maintain your stance regardless of the negative reactions (the attitude, the rolling of eyes, the silent treatment, etc.) from those who were expecting you to say yes, and you disappointed them by saying no.**

I hope I have challenged you to turn off the autopilot of your life and land your plane, self, in order to properly nurture your emotional, mental, and physical needs before your next departure. What I desire the most for you to gather from this chapter and the chapters following is attending to self should always be made a priority, especially when giving of yourself to others is a natural expectation. Knowing your limits and setting boundaries will save you from over-exertion and most definitely from compromising the authenticity of self. Self-maintenance is the key to preserving one's body, mind, and emotions. As we go on this journey together, you will discover that the principles introduced throughout this book are designed to teach you how to consistently deposit life back into your life so that when withdrawals are made from those around you, you will not become depleted. So, let's proceed forward.

Reflection Questions

1. Do you find it difficult to say no? If yes, why? If no, why?

Reflection Questions

2. What part of you, Self, is lost in the mix as a result of constantly attending to the needs of others?

Chapter 2

THE MIND, THE MIND, THE MIND

There is no way around it. We all do it, and that is Think. The ability to think is not only powerful but an intrinsic attribute of our humanist nature. According to Dr. Caroline Leaf, "Thoughts are measurable and occupy mental 'real estate.' Thoughts are active; they grow and change. Thoughts influence every decision, word, action, and physical reaction we make" (Leaf, 2009, p.13). Our thoughts are constantly being influenced either by past experiences, repetitive information, and/or experiences of others - all of which shape our mindset or what I call the inner perception of life (your reality of life). Your mindset, your inner perception of life, is visibly displayed either through your actions and the words that come out of your mouth.

Your thought life, the way you think, is highly relevant from the standpoint that the more hats you wear, the higher the demand placed on your life. The higher the demand placed on your life, the more crucial it is for you to infuse your mind with words of substance while exposing your mind to people, places, and things capable of sending messages (verbally and/or nonverbally) that will reinforce strong, positive, and stable thinking. That is why it is pertinent to connect to people who are like minded. In other words, you must be diligent in harnessing your thoughts so that you can be aware of what is expected of you from each hat worn. What you allow to consume your thoughts, or better yet, what you allow to rent space in your mind, will dictate your performance level in fulfilling your duties, your obligations to those around you. Thoughts geared towards being productive, responsible, giving, and non-judgmental are unleashed through your actions and directly imparted into the lives of those who are the recipient of the wisdom, protection, love, and guidance associated with the hat or hats being worn by you. For example, as a mother I am cognizant of who or what I expose my mind to in regard to raising my daughter. Being a parent is a very sensitive matter. Outsiders, including family members, who present negativity to me, either through comments/criticism and/or suggestions that go against the gradient of what I hold to be true about my parenting, I immediately block. I take preventive measures (i.e., reflecting on positive thoughts regarding parenthood) by barring those unfruitful words from entering my mind and disturbing the existing thoughts that bolster my ability of being a good parent. So, my advice to you is, do not allow your mind to become a landfill where people can dump their negativity. It is vital for you to guard what goes into your eye gate and ear gate because your thoughts will affect your emotions, and your emotions will trigger your feelings. Ultimately, your feelings will dictate to your behavior, negative or positive. The bottom line is this, you being successful in effectively operating within the role or roles of each hat or hats worn is based on the condition of your mind and emotions. With that being said, this chapter will cover the following: 1) which habitual mindsets to avoid; 2) which mindset best undergirds your many hats; 3) how to manage your thought life; and 4) who and what to avoid when harnessing one's thoughts.

A Mindset That Can Undergird Your Hats

Is it possible to have a mindset that is capable of undergirding the many hats that you wear each and every day? Most definitely! You will find that possessing what I call an undeviating mindset is a game changer. An undeviating mindset is an unwavering, steady thought process that is programmed by words that create mental images that are in agreement with the purpose and mission behind the hat or hats being worn. This particular mindset requires both determination and diligence in order to develop and maintain a thought process that is equipped to do the following: 1) Stay connected or in tune to the purpose of the hat being worn. When you do not know the purpose of a thing, you lack the ability to not only appreciate its existence, but also how to effectively operate within its existence, 2) Reflect on the words and actions that bring to life the many hats you wear, and 3) Believe in or be in agreement with your ability to confidently wear your hat as a mother, teacher, entrepreneur, etc., while serving those who constantly draw from what has been deposited on the inside of you - leadership, wisdom, guidance, nurturing, love, inner strength, discernment, organization, instruction, or counsel. WARNING! There will always be someone out there who intentionally or unintentionally tries to pare down your confidence level as a result of their own personal fears, jealousy, or misunderstanding of the significance behind the hat being worn. Having confidence is a must from the standpoint that it will always push you forward; on the other hand, insecurities will always keep you at a standstill.

Possessing this type of mindset, an undeviating mindset, calls for a mental allegiance on your behalf which refuses to settle for a mindset that is vulnerable, easily distracted, and/ or in opposition with the purpose and the mission of the many hats you wear in life. An undeviating mindset, if employed on a regular basis, will bring order to your thought process so that you can override negativity, self-inflicted limitations set by others, and even life challenges. You may say, "Sheryl, why is it so important to operate from undeviating mindset?" Wearing many hats, occupying multiple positions, requires you to have order and structure in your life, and that includes having order in your thought life. Let me reemphasize, your pattern of thinking has a significant impact on the way you respond to life, both privately and publicly. My "gym associate" Harrington (a.k.a "Boston") summed it up so beautifully by saying, "Success comes by disciplining one's thoughts. People in general want to succeed in life, but they are not willing to do what it takes to be successful. One of the dos of success is letting go of thoughts that are capable of paralyzing an individual's ability to mentally migrate towards productive thoughts that affirm one's success both personally and professionally."

Habitual Mindsets to Avoid

Let's contemplate "what if" for a brief moment. What happens when you deprive your mind the rest it needs by failing to disconnect from the hustle and bustle of everyday life? If your thoughts are always scattered, how effective are you? What would happen if you did not set aside time to reprogram your mind in order to combat the negativity that tries to bombard your thoughts from being in sync with the purpose of the hat being worn? What ifs can be all of our reality if we choose to ignore how sensitive, how vulnerable, and even how naive our mind can be if not properly tamed or programmed to serve rather than lead.

No one ever said developing an undeviating mindset would be an easy task. The truth of the matter is this particular thought process requires daily maintenance or what is commonly referred to as reprogramming the mind. Our mind lacks the ability to self-regulate itself to stay on course due to fact that there is so much out there competing for its attention - social media, current affairs, families and friends' drama, and the overall negativity we experience throughout the day. As a result, we must be sensitive to not only what we allow into our eye gate and ear gate but also what we allow to come out of our mouth for the simple reason that the mind is so vulnerable and will easily attach itself to information that is harmful rather than beneficial. A preschool teacher told me how her brother would always degrade his daughter by telling her she was stupid and would never amount to anything in life. These negative words took root and began to shape not only her thoughts but behavior to the point that she made bad decisions in life. The good news is that this young lady is making positive changes in her life through her counseling sessions as she continues to confront the lie that was forcefully imparted in her life that she would never amount to anything. The only conclusion I came to regarding her father's insensitivity is that he was unable to speak words of life into his daughter because he did not have it in himself to give. In other words, you can only give what you have.

Let's be real, when our thoughts are properly being guided and pro-tected, we are more happy, confident, and productive throughout the day. However, a mind that has no restraints will have you thinking that you are a failure, unattractive, incomplete, incompetent, and even unqualified to serve those who withdraw from the hat or hats you were called to wear. And if that is not enough, there are those off the wall thoughts that will make you say, "Where did that come from?" These thoughts will land in the canvas of your imagination trying to convince you, through your emotions, that those negative words are true. Oh, the mind will try to take you places where you may have no desire to go if left to roam. Ladies, we are women of purpose, so it is a must that you and I be diligent in transforming our thoughts so that the greatness that is on the inside of us can properly grow and mature and eventually impact the lives of others. Let's briefly explore the three types of mindsets that are at odds with the undeviating mindset and therefore, should be avoided at all times.

The Dull Mind

Just the thought of having to think about or remember one more thing can be a chore within itself, especially when the responsibilities of life and/or the care of those who are connected to the many hats you wear are constantly pulling or tugging on you to respond. So, a dull mindset, in essence, is a mental overload that is the byproduct of feeling pressured to think beyond what you are capable of handling. In other words, the mind is bombarded with so much stuff that a mental break is much needed in order to bring it back to a healthy concentration level. If operating from a dull mindset continues, frustration, depression, stress, and fatigue, just to name a few, will set in and begin to orchestrate one's physical and emotional state of being.

When you are mentally overloaded, you forfeit your ability to:

1. **follow your heart, decreasing your ability to make sound decisions.**

2. **recognize pertinent information and words of wisdom, warning signs that are beneficial to your growth and protection.**

3. **not only address your needs but the needs of others.**

4. **fully enjoy those priceless moments in life, such as celebrations, unexpected opportunities and/or accomplishments.**

5. **recall.**

Complacent Mindset

The second mind set to avoid is that of complacency. A complacent mindset is composed of thoughts that are centered around being settled or in common with not only the role currently being occupied but also content with receiving the same results. The best question that would describe a complacent mentality is, "Everything is ok as is, so why it is necessary to change?" As a result, there is no inner desire to challenge one's thought process to think beyond the norm or out of the box in effort to take the role or roles connected to the hat being worn to another level. A complacent mindset will always keep an individual stuck in neutral causing her to either consciously or unconsciously reject innovative ideas, words of wisdom, and constructive criticism that could potentially be the solution to accelerating in life. Remember, personal growth is not an option, especially when the hats you wear are impacting those around you.

An Entertaining Mindset

An entertaining mindset should never become an option for women who wear many hats. This mindset consists of being mentally occupied with multiple thoughts that are constantly competing for acknowledgement and response. An entertaining mindset can be the most tiresome thought process there is from the standpoint that it may disrupt one's ability to concentrate on thoughts that undergird peace, productivity, honesty, and one's purpose in life, but it can also become taxing both emotionally and physically. Granted, an entertaining mindset can be a carrier of purposeful thoughts, but it mainly carries the channels that play distracting thoughts (i.e., thoughts of being a failure, reflecting on past mistakes, etc.). As a result, if distracting thoughts and purposeful thoughts are not properly sorted through and separated, purposeful thoughts will eventually be outnumbered by distracting thoughts, causing the following things to occur: 1) distracting thoughts will begin to drown out purposeful thoughts (or thinking) to the point that your purpose is no longer considered as being valuable, truthful, and/or an option on how to conduct oneself accordingly; 2) distracting thoughts will take root in an individual's belief system and begin to shape her reality of life. As a result, distracting thoughts will start influencing one's behavior both publicly and/or privately, and 3) frustration, anxiety, fear, shame and guilt, depression, and even anger becomes the platform of one's life because there are no "mental rules" on what a person should or should not be thinking about. The lack of enforcing "mental rules" can cause a person's overall well-being to become stagnant. Ladies, we may not be able to stop an unwarranted thought from visiting our minds, but we sure can determine how long it stays. Rule of thumb: one, think about what you are thinking about and how it will have an impact on you and those who are connected to the hat you wear. Second, always replace disruptive thoughts with productive thoughts so that you can see where you are going and know what to do once you get there.

Managing Your Thought Life

The success behind wearing your assigned hat or hats with confidence is your ability to diligently manage your thought life. When I think of styling a hat with confidence, I can recall as a child going to church with my family on Sunday mornings. As I entered the sanctuary, I was visually captivated by the array of colorful, uniquely designed hats eloquently worn with confidence by the women in the congregation. The hat itself did not produce confidence; rather, it was how the women perceived themselves before, during, and after showcasing their Sunday hats, which conveyed the message of being confident in who they were. An individual who trains his or her mindset to think above distracting thoughts will not only experience confidence but also peace, clarity, creativity, joy, productivity, and a passion to impact the lives of others. While on the other hand, an individual who allows their mind to be governed by distracting thoughts will always be weighed down by uncertainties and emotional instabilities. Both (uncertainties and emotional instabilities) suppress one's confidence level. Believe it or not, you are what you think; how you think will determine how you will respond to life, and how you respond to life will reveal if you are mastering life or if life is mastering you. With this being said, mental breaks should never be considered as an option that sometimes you do and sometimes you don't practice, but rather mental breaks should become a lifestyle. The benefit of mental breaks is that it allows you to step away and disconnect from decisions, commitments, and people in general in order to settle once and for all the lies and imaginary misconceptions that stem from distracting thoughts. Reprogramming your mind daily keeps those negative thoughts at bay that are notorious for interfering with your making sound decisions for your life. Daily reprogramming also protects those who are impacted by the many hats you wear. Mental breaks, if done consistently and properly, will fuel your confidence level, causing you to wear your hats more securely while fulfilling your roles in life. Note: I know that this may seem like a lot, but I assure you, when you are calm, you are more productive than when you are under stress. Being calm or stressed is a choice; it is all in how you think. I recommend that you employ the following mental break regiments: 1), grateful moments, 2) power naps; and 3) confronting and replacing distracting thoughts. You will find that each break is designed to put you both mentally and emotionally in a good place so that you feel refreshed (rejuvenated), strengthened, motivated, and focused when resuming your designated role or roles. So, never deny your mind the "spa treatment" (mental break) it needs to effectively serve you in the midst of you serving others.

Grateful Moments

Grateful moments are just that - moments of being grateful. This particular mental break involves embracing moments which effortlessly put you and me in remembrance of what we already have. I like to refer this as being thankful. For example, I am grateful for my family. I am grateful that I have a place to call home. I am grateful for good health and soundness of mind. I am grateful that I have a place of employment. The list can go on and on. Grateful moments, being thankful, bring a sense of ease to your mind as it departs from thoughts that breed feelings of being rushed, discontent, overwhelmed, anxious, and/or uncertain, therefore allowing the mind to reset as it begins to ponder on positive, uplifting thoughts. From my own personal experience, grateful moments also provide the following:

1. **They serve as a sedative to your emotions, calming the emotions so that they are not left navigating your day. Your emotions were designed to follow and not to lead. Rule of thumb, negative emotions trigger feelings that will try to distract you or make it seem like it's a struggle to be committed to yourself but also those around you. Positive emotions are more prone to trigger feelings that keep you more anchored when depositing into the lives of others.**

2. **Grateful moments keep you content and appreciative for what you currently have (i.e., family, friends, etc.). I make it a habit to have grateful moments throughout the day. I have discovered that my strongest moments are when I am driving long distance or jogging. As I reflect and voice what I am grateful for (i.e., "I am so thank for my family, etc.), my mind and emotions become in sync with each other. It is when my emotions and mind are in**

harmony with each other that I am able to be more productive and less nonproductive, and,

3. **Grateful moments strategically put you in a position where you are mentally receptive when favor, promotion, and opportunities manifest in your life. In other words, grateful moments acclimate you to receiving as opposed to rejecting when things are added to your life.**

Power Naps

The second mental break is the mighty power nap. A power nap is one of the most powerful ways to rejuvenate the mind throughout the course of the day. However, naps are the least used relaxation technique due to the fact that people are always on the go, blending in with the hustle and bustle of life, which causes people to neglect the mind and body the proper rest it needs to serve them effectively. Experts have concluded that incorporating naps during the day can diminish stress and reduce the risk of heart attack, increasing alertness, brightening your mood, boosting memory enhancing creativity, and improving perception, stamina, motor skills, and accuracy (WebMD, 2020).

You may say, "I do not have time to take a nap! And I say, "You cannot afford not to take one, so make time!" If it is just 10-15 minutes in your car on your lunch break or reclining in your chair, close your eyes and allow your mind to shift or ease into the pause mode before reconvening with your day. You may think taking a nap or naps will put you behind schedule, but au contraire, naps release the energy and rest needed both physically and mentally in order to keep you on task.

Confronting and Replacing Distracting Thoughts

As long as you exist here on this earth, you have thoughts that make you say, "Where did that come from?" I have found that distracting thoughts are basically the byproduct of the residue left behind from a certain scene or scenes watched on television and/or movies (including the news), negative words or behavior meant to cause harm or embarrassment, and/or past experiences. Distracting thoughts could become one's reality if it entertained for a long period of time. As I indicated earlier, the mind does not know the difference between real and not real, so if distracting thoughts are not eradicated immediately, they will eventually have just as much relevance as thoughts that are true, of good report, affirming, and meaningful, and that should not be.

So, how do we as women confront and replace distracting thoughts that are seemingly on a mission to distort the many hats we wear in life? It is a mixture of those grateful moments, timely naps, along with purposeful words, that properly insulate the canvas of your imagination in order to make it difficult for distracting thoughts to seep through and disrupt the creativity, flow, discipline, the correct visual image, organization, and tranquility which is represented through the actions displayed when operating within the capacity of each hat you wear in life. For instance, I settle my mind before taking a nap by reminiscing on all that I am grateful for that day. Then, I softly verbalize purposeful words and/or statements (i.e., "I am not destined to fail, but succeed in life.") until my mind is at ease, and I slip off into a peaceful nap. I am reinforcing the insulation around my mind so that distracting thoughts will not penetrate through to present to me something that is not true. Remember, your ability to wear your hat or hats effectively is based on how you think. Now, go find you a quiet place and pull out a pillow and blanket and take a nap. You will be the better for it.

Assignment

1. What distracting thoughts have been taunting you for a
    long time?

Assignment

2. What type of mindset do you need to avoid, and why?

Assignment

3. If you took time out to properly insulate the canvas of your imagination, how would your life be different?

Assignment

4. What are you grateful for?

Chapter 3

COMPARING HATS IS A NO-NO!

It amazes me the number of women who are obsessed with comparing themselves to others. This addictive competitive mentality is spreading rapidly among us as women, to the point that our deeply hidden thoughts are now being publicly unleashed, exposing our insecurities, inadequacies, misconceptions, fears, and jealousy through our actions. As a result, we are held captive to our thoughts, which not only hinders us from embracing our uniqueness but also distracts us from staying in our lane, where our gifts and talents flourish the most.

"Beauty shop" talk was taking place one Friday evening. As the renowned motivational speaker was sitting in the chair getting her hair styled for the next speaking engagement, she asked her hair stylist, who was known for her words of wisdom, "Why does it seem like women automatically show signs of jealousy even before I open my mouth to speak?" The hair stylist pondered while placing the rollers strategically in her client's hair. The stylist then proceeded by saying, "Women in general compare themselves to other women based on the level of their overall well-being in life - emotionally, mentally, socially, financially, and academically. They have created customized lenses made up of insecurities, inadequacies, fears, past failures, and prejudices, having the potential to do the following:

1. **Reflect on self and the area in which one lacks, therefore interfering with progress,**

2. **Justify one's critical opinion towards the woman who appears to have it all together,**

3. **Find a "But" i.e., "She is a beauty but she's really short!" in an attempt to tarnish the image or character of the individual indirectly or directly. This "But" is an attempt to pacify their perceived shortcomings against the image of a woman who has diligently created an image for herself, and**

4. **Stroke one's superior mentality.**

Believe or not, there are people out there who think that they are better than others. However, when someone comes across the 'untouchable's' path whose appearance and professionalism is at a whole different level, he or she will either duck and hide in order to avoid giving a compliment, ambush the individual with her verbal resume that entails a list of her endless achievements, or intentionally fail to acknowledge the presence of the individual altogether." I have come to the conclusion that an individual who is obsessed with being superior is controlled by fear. I will elaborate more regarding being fear-based within the framework of this chapter.

Ladies, this is going to be another deep chapter. The time has finally come for me to expose this wilderness experience, comparing oneself to others in relation to their current situation. It has left many women wondering helplessly as they are being led by their insecurities, fears, shame, guilt, and prejudices to point that they are unable to focus on their mission in life. So, let's dig deep, and somewhere within the pages of this chapter find the self that needs to be exposed and addressed so that you can move forward and successfully run the race which has been set before you.

Compare vs Admire

I dare not assume that everyone knows the difference between compare and admire. If everyone knew the difference between the two, then the chances of being jealous and/or envious would be minimal. Those of us who diligently wear our many hats in life will always be subject to being examined by others who either wish they had, wonder why you have, and/or believe what they have is better. So, what does it actually mean to compare oneself to another? Comparing oneself to another is operating within the arena of competitiveness. The individual mentally begins to look at the similarities and/or differences between self and the other person to the point that he or she creates expectations that may not be suitable for his or her lifestyle. For example, let's say Amanda occasionally logs in on social media to see what is going on in the lives of her colleagues. While browsing, Amanda sees that many of her colleagues have done quite well for themselves. Unaware of what was taking place, Amanda was subtly being lured into the arena of competitiveness, where she began to compare her life to others, arousing her emotions and feelings that were better off not being disturbed.

When an individual makes it a habit of comparing oneself to others, she forfeits her opportunity to learn from the stories behind others' success. I had an opportunity to meet a woman who was beautiful on the inside as well as the outside by the name of Sunshine. She works as a cashier at a prominent neighborhood grocery store here in Georgia. While I purchased groceries, I had the pleasure of hearing the condensed version of Sunshine's remarkable story of overcoming a severe illness. She indicated that I was looking at a miracle and then proceeded to say that people can only see the "now" of her life, but if they only knew all that it took - the strength. courage, and determination for her to arrive at the now, they would be amazed. Not only does Sunshine's impeccable persona resonate throughout her place of employment, but she also wears the hat of an encourager when she regularly visits stroke victims at a well-known hospital in Atlanta, Georgia. Sunshine's ideology is "people will never know what you have gone through in life unless you share."

The action of choice when wearing many hats is to admire those who carry the mantel of a mentor, those whom you can draw from as they pour into your life wisdom, words of encouragement, guidance, and lessons learned from both their personal and professional experiences. To admire someone is totally different from comparing oneself to another from the standpoint that an individual puts herself in a teachable position to learn or pull from the knowledge, expertise, creativity, and the charismatic disposition possessed by the one being admired. To admire adds to self, whereas to compare takes away from self. To admire encourages self, whereas to compare discourages self. To admire affirms self, whereas to compare questions self. To admire is open to change, whereas to compare resist change. The new version of you will admire and not compare.

The Character of One to be Admired

I hope I have induced you thus far to be an admirer rather than a comparer. It is profitable to be admirer, for it allows you to gain a better understanding of not only the assignment behind the many hats you wear but also how to wear them confidently. You will discover the many hats you wear in life will require you to not only be an admirer but also to be admired by those around you and even those whom you come in contact with. However, whether you are admiring or being admired, you should not lose sight of your primary purpose, which is impacting the lives of those who are under your watch. In other words, refrain from getting caught up in the recognition based on your title, but stay focused on your mission. I believe that is worth repeating: refrain from getting caught up in the recognition based on your title, but stay focused on your mission.

What qualifies a person to be admired by others? Is it their charisma, experience, compassion, "je ne sais quoi" ? No doubt, all of these traits are noteworthy, but what surpasses them all is an individual's character. One's character, moral disposition, is voiced through his or her actions or response during different life situations. An individual's character not only reveals who she is as a person, but it many cases, it determines how effective she is in fulfilling the role of roles associated with the many hats she wears. I say in many cases because you really don't get to know a person until you spend time with them. Sadly, there are people who have seemingly mastered their ability to hide their shady character. But how many of you know that whatever is corrupt or shady will eventually come to light? You may be wondering, what does this have to with creating a new version of you? A lot! We were not designed to admire ourselves; rather, we were designed to learn from our surroundings and from those who we either interact with on a daily basis, periodically, and/or once in a lifetime. Think about it, what if a child only learns from himself or herself? This would set limitations on his or her abilities to properly grow and develop. Well, the same applies to you - there is more than you to learn from. You may wear the hat of mother or teacher with excellence, but there is always someone out there who has taken the concept and practice of motherhood or educator to another level that you could learn a few pointers from. "Well, Sheryl, I do not need to learn from others. What can they teach me?" Now you are operating in pride. Pride is infamous for persuading people to deny those who are under their leadership the opportunity to be blanketed with the knowledge that would be gained if they had only humbled themselves and received from someone qualified to be admired.

During the process of depositing back into yourself as you create this new version of you, I strongly recommend that you reevaluate your character to determine if it is healthy or not. Why? 1) Your character needs to be genuine so that it can properly undergird your overall well-being; 2) Your character amplifies your ability to perform your duties in addition to carrying out the decisions associated with the role or roles you currently occupy, and 3) Your moral disposition helps regulate both your intrapersonal and interpersonal relationships.

Let's briefly look at the benefits of having a healthy character.

1. **Healthy character attracts respect.**

2. **Healthy character attracts favor. People will do things for you that they will not do for others.**

3. **Healthy character causes people to value not only your wisdom and knowledge, but also to incorporate what they have learned readily.**

4. **Healthy character will persuade you to make decisions that are beneficial for the well-being of those who you deposit into daily.**

5. **Healthy character will make you less likely to succumb to temptations that make you compromise what you hold to be true.**

6. **Healthy character becomes the attire for an individual who is people-centered as opposed to self-centered.**

7. **Healthy character directs you towards your destiny as opposed to detouring you.**

Story

A close friend of mine described her past work environment as being a place infested with people whose character was beyond shady. From the administrator to the supervisor and everyone in between, they either lied, cheated, manipulated, gossiped, and/or stole pertinent information all for the sake of rising to the top or being accepted. The few whose character was intact or healthy were sadly outnumbered by the "shady mob." The moral disposition of this particular cultural organization eventually negated the mission of the university along with other administration issues, causing the entire university to close permanently. Those who were held responsible for wearing the hat of serving as a liaison for both the instructors and students got the short end of the stick because of others' selfish motives.

Thought-Provoking Questions

1. What do you find yourself doing the most comparing or admiring? Why?

Thought-Provoking Questions

2. What is it about your character that will either have a positive or negative influence over those who are connected to the many hats you wear?

Thought-Provoking Questions

3. If someone was admiring you, what would they learn?

Chapter 4

REMOVING THE TOXICITY OUT OF YOUR LIFE

Have you ever at some point in time in your life been subjected to toxicity? Whether it be emotional, social, mental, physical, moral, and/or relational, toxins are acclaimed for gradually seizing into one's territory of life and setting up camp. Toxicity will create an environment where negativity grows at a fast pace, making it difficult but not impossible for external (home remedies, medical services, new friends, counseling, etc.) and internal (proper amount of rest) solutions to assist in reclaiming one's territory in order to operate from a healthy environment as you fulfill your purpose in life. Sadly, many people have become enslaved by the toxicity that currently resides in their lives to the point that they dodge the process of making changes for fear that it might not work.

Toxins have no boundaries. They are not biased; they will conform to anyone allowing them entrance and residence. For over 19 years, a well-educated, successful career woman endured a toxic relationship by staying in the home for the sake of her child having both a father and mother. She is one of the sweetest, most loving, and giving persons you every want to meet. She took pride in the many hats she wore and diligently fulfilled her obligations accordingly. She was not only beautiful on the inside but also the outside. If given the opportunity, a good man would have cherished her and treated her like the queen she was. Instead, she married a man who constantly depreciated her value as a woman, mother, and wife. Rather than blanketing Carmen with love, encouragement, and validation, he smothered her with negativity and neglect. If that was not enough, he had the nerve to have an affair during their marriage. There is much more to this story, but the point I want to make is that while Carmen tolerated being in a toxic relationship for the sake of her daughter, her emotional, mental, and physical health suffered the consequence as a result of her decision to stay married to her husband. You may have heard a story like this one or you may be that "story." Whatever the case may be, at one time or another, we all can stand a good cleansing to remove all toxins that try to invade our overall well-being. These toxins compete for our energy, positive stance, and the concentration needed to wear our hats effectively. As we plunge into this chapter, we are going to learn how to patrol our thoughts, emotions, relationships, health, and character, so that unwarranted toxins will not dominate over our lives. This chapter will cover the following: 1) defining toxic, 2) the signs of toxicity, and 3) detoxing from toxins.

Defining Toxic

What does the word toxic mean? Toxic is defined as being "poisonous, extremely harsh, malicious, harmful, or exhibiting symptoms of infection" ("Definition of toxic," 2022). Now let me emphasize some key words in this definition – "poisonous, extremely harsh, and malicious," - so that I can put my twist on the word toxicity. Toxicity, when given access by way of negative thoughts, words, burdensome relationships, stress, worry, fear, unforgiveness, shame, or guilt, begins to develop into a merciless, poisonous, extremely harsh, malicious infection that has no concept of boundaries. Spreading through one's mind, emotions, relationships, work environment, etc., until it destroys everything that resembles healthy. This may sound complex, and it is, but it is a must that we be good stewards over our bodies, minds, and emotions so that toxins do not invade our lives and those who are connected to the many hats we wear.

Signs of Toxicity

If you do not expose a thing, how will you ever know that it exists? There are women from all walks of life who are clueless to the fact that their overall well-being is toxic, and they are in desperate need of a good detox. Let's examine the signs of toxicity that can be enveloped within the area of one's mind, emotions, morals, and relationships. I challenge you to be honest with yourself in order to see where you may fit within this diagnostic profile. The healing process begins when you are open to change.

1. **Difficulties in concentration. The inability to concentrate or stay focused on the task at hand is a sure sign of toxicity. An individual's reality of life is consumed with negativity to the point that there is low visibility.**

2. **Inability to forgive. Unable, and for many, unwilling to show mercy towards oneself or others due to past acts/experiences that either caused hurt, humiliation, or disappointment. To envelope one's thoughts, feelings, and emotions around the past to the point that shame, guilt, and/or resentment begin to dictate one's perception of self and others.**

3. **Tendency to complain. Can never be satisfied. Lacking the ability to appreciate what one has, but always wanting more to find that it is still not enough.**

4. **Isolation. Separating oneself from people, places, and/or things that are not only influential in the positive changes that have occurred in one's life but also supportive in providing insight regarding an individual's purpose in life. Isolation becomes a**

consideration when the following things occur: 1) Life challenges have caused an individual to surrender and give up fighting; 2) Old behaviors, thoughts, and/or relationships that are detrimental to the individual's overall well-being are rekindled; 3) Feelings of failing self and others occur; and 4) Burn-out sparks. Toxins have taken over an individual's life to the point that he or she has dismissed himself or herself from others, creating their own "island" of self-pity. If an individual remains on this island too long, the temptation to entertain and even participate in unhealthy habits can prolong the lifespan of the existing toxins.

5. Fatigue. One's energy is exerted, allowing toxins to gain entrance through the following ways: 1) Over-exerting self. Being everything to everybody and never taking the time out to take care of self, 2) Flirting with thoughts that compromise your character, keeping you in constant fear and/or limiting your ability to see beyond where you currently are. In other words, toxins, if allowed, will self-appoint themselves as the artist of your canvas of imagination and 3) Being unsettled. Thoughts are going in every direction, putting the individual in an indecisive position.

6. Vulnerable mindset. Easily persuaded to believe what others believe even when it contradicts one's beliefs. Toxicity can cause an individual to become mentally lethargic to the point that their convictions are being challenged as they consider the suggestions, options, and/or negative comments presented by others. For example, Lakeland is adamant

about starting her own business once she graduates in June with her business degree. Her desire of being a successful entrepreneur is more real than her current position in life. However, one day while at work, Lakeland, in all her excitement concerning her new endeavors, reveals a little more than she normally would regarding her next phase in life. As a result, one of her coworkers, the dream killer, begins to downsize Lakeland's plans and tells her that she will never make it outside of corporate America. Lakeland leaves the break room not only a little unsettled, but she finds herself entertaining the fear of failing if she leaves her current job to pursue her own business. Lakeland is becoming vulnerable to the toxins that were injected into her thoughts by way of the disbelief, jealousy, and lack of vision from someone on the outside.

7. Excuses. Creating all the reasons in the world why one cannot be who he or she needs to be for self as well as for others.

8. The Fear of What People are Thinking About Me. This toxic symptom weighs heavily on an individual's mind, causing the person to be anxious and/or fearful as a result of constantly being preoccupied with what others think about him or her. The person experiences overwhelming feelings of discomfort while in public because they fear that all eyes are on them as people mentally judge them.

Detoxification

If you have ever gone through a detoxification process, it is just that, a process. This cleansing method is usually not designed to complete its mission overnight, but it is a gradual process which attempts to not only eradicate impurities that have accumulated in one's physical body over a period of time but also to bring the physical body back to its original state for a healthier function. I am quite aware that the detoxification process is more medically in-depth than what I am presenting to you, but my goal is to challenge you to put equal importance on detoxifying your thought life, emotions, character, and/or relationship with self and others just like you would detoxifying your physical body. In other words, you should always place high value on your thought life, emotional state, moral disposition, and how you relate to self and others. Why? The many hats you wear in life require you to be mentally, emotionally, socially, morally, and physically balanced so that you operate at your optimal potential. Toxicity, if not properly dealt with, will weigh down your hat or hats, making it difficult for you to wear and fulfill your responsibilities effectively. Here is a list of some safeguards or detoxification antidotes that I personally incorporate in my life in order to prevent or negate toxins from setting up camp in my mind and then dispersing themselves throughout other areas of my life.

Detox 1:

Being Delivered from People

I put this one first because I have found that people are really struggling in this area. Being held captive by people's thoughts is one of the most dangerous toxins anyone could ever experience. Imagine someone constantly "pairing" their mind, like pairing a cell phone to a car, to those they come in contact with, in wonderment of what others are thinking about them. This toxic behavior puts an individual at the mercy of others to determine their destiny in life, diluting one's confidence in knowing who she is, what she is capable of doing and having in life. So, how do you rid yourself of this particular toxin? 1) Each day tell yourself the following: "I will not bear the fear of what people are thinking about me." Meaning, refuse to allow yourself to be discomfited by the belief that what people think or say about you could possibly become a reality. 2) Refrain from making it a habit of locking eyes with people and/ or looking at people's facial expressions in hopes of approval or wondering what they are thinking about you. I like to say that most of the people that you are concerned about are uncertain about what they think about themselves. And if they are thinking, speaking, and looking at you in a negative way, do not let it rent space in your mind, and 3) Before leaving the house, make sure that your mind is in the mission mode. Visualize yourself successfully doing all that is required of you for that day. Someone that makes it a priority to be mission-minded is less likely to "pair" their mind with distractions.

Detox 2:

Solidify Your Internal World

There are some homes that are better insulated than others. What determines if a house is well-insulated or not is its ability to seal in heat during the wintertime and release heat during those unbearable summer months. In other words, is your home internally equipped (well-insulated) to combat outside elements? Well, just like a home must be internally equipped – must be made strong, efficient, and stable to withstand outside elements, your internal world (thoughts, emotions, and inner image) should be stronger, clearer, and more stable than the outside world you face on a daily basis.

Here are the following detox sealants needed to close off all entrances in order to prevent toxins from under-insulating your internal world/reality: 1) Keep your mind fastened on things that are positive, productive, peaceful, and honest when in the company of people. This prevents toxic thoughts (i.e., being a failure, reliving a messy situation, etc.) from dropping down into your thoughts in search for a space to rent in your mind. Make up in your mind that you have no vacancies for toxic thoughts. 2) Speak words that will undergird, strengthen, and reaffirm your internal world. For example, "I am destined for success." "Giving up is not an option for me." "I am a masterpiece and not just a work of art." "I am valuable." "My existence here on earth is significant." "My presence demands an explanation." "Seeds of greatness are on the inside of me." "I choose to have a positive impact on those around me." When your internal world resonates with words of substance, it weakens toxins (i.e., stress, challenges of life, sarcasm, etc.) from penetrating into your internal world and causing havoc in your life. In addition, speaking words of substance disciplines you to avoid the temptation of being governed by your emotions. Finally, speaking positive words that reflect your internal world creates a mental billboard which advertises what you believe and how to choose to respond to life.

Detox 3:

Stop Telling Your Business!

Have you noticed that our society is consumed with being nosy? People, in general, feel privileged or entitled to know the intrinsic details of your life, with or without your permission. It appears privacy, in all that it stands for, is becoming more and more distinct while social media surges like never before. Social media has eroded to the degree that privacy is the antithesis of transparency. Let me cut to the chase: make it your business to stop telling people all your business so that they cannot run your business. In other words, refrain from giving people free access to your life, especially when it opens the door for others to prejudge or manipulate you to prove a point, to belittle, or to compare themselves to you. Here are some responses I or my friends have used to address those who take pleasure in prying into people's lives: 1) Practice the art of being silent. Sometimes, ok, many times it is best to be of few words when among people, especially among those you do not know. Silence enhances your listening skills; it allows you the opportunity to gather information needed to make a sound decision. The art of silence even strengthens your ability to discern the good and not so good intentions of those you come in contact with; and finally, silence becomes the safeguard to your privacy. My girlfriend Gayle has mastered the art of silence. She said, "When people try to pry into my personal business that they are not privileged to know, I simply do not acknowledge the question or questions being asked: rather, I change the conversation." Some people may say that's rude. Au contraire, it is rude when someone continues to reframe the question in multiple ways in an attempt to force information from you. There are four things I live by: 1) Always protect your heart and mind, 2) Refuse to let people pin you in a corner and pressure you to answer questions just to satisfy their inquisitive behavior, 3) Silence is an answer also, and 4) Verbal modesty is not a crime. Let's be real, there are some questions that have the ability to resurface; toxins that were once dealt with in the past can reemerge. Let me reiterate, if you feel any inklings that your emotions and thoughts are navigating back to an unhealthy place in your life, usher people out of your business with a quickness by telling them, "I am uncomfortable with the question that you are asking me and I choose not to respond." If they get offended, they will be alright. At least your resolve of not being willing to participate in satisfying others' curiosity cravings was not compromised. Once you start telling people all your business, they will want to run your business. There is room for only one boss in your store.

Detox 4:

Forgive and Release

Another seemingly difficult toxin for people to dismiss from their lives is unforgiveness. "You do not know what they have done to me." Or, "I can never forgive myself!" Whether it be what others have done to you or if it is self-inflicted, either way, unforgiveness if one of the harshest toxins anyone could every experience in life.

Why? Because unforgiveness shows no mercy on how one thinks, feels, and/or reacts towards self and others. If that is not enough, unforgiveness has its own "remote" that plays hurt, betrayal, disappointment, and failure over and over again. This "remote" increases pain, stirs up strife, and even creates a security blanket that is embroidered with shame, guilt, and resentment. Finally, unforgiveness forfeits an individual's ability to successfully wear her many hats as they are meant to be worn. Invisible walls - distrust, distancing oneself from others and/or negative comments or responses toward others - secretly eat away at the core of one's overall well-being. As an act of your will, make up in your mind once and for all that you will not be held emotionally and mentally captive to someone who has wrongfully done you wrong in the past. You will no longer set up camp and roast "woe is me" marshmallows now that the expiration date has expired. Yes, what happened to you is real; it was unfair and in many cases a tragedy, but you have to move forward so that the healing process can be put into motion. This detoxification process is ignited once you release that person and move out of the past and into the future so those who are connected to the many hats you wear get all of you and not just half of you. Don't be so attached to your past that you do not recognize who you are today.

Detox 5:

Walking Away from Toxic People, Places or Things

It amazes me what women have held on to, even me, that have toxicity written all over it. There are people, places, or things that should never been given the opportunity to flirt with our mind nor emotions. If you look back, the time spent holding on to toxic relationships, socializing at venomous places, and/or participating in negative addictive activities could have been utilized in a more productive manner. We may not be able to erase our past, but we sure can learn from it. I believe the theme for each and every one of our lives should be getting clarity, and once clarity is received, then growing from what one has learned, I will never forget my baby brother giving me these words of advice. He said, "Sheryl, our lives are like a freeway, and many times we may get off the wrong exits in life (i.e., unhealthy relationships, etc.), causing hurts, disappointments, shame, guilt, and/or grief. Get right back on the freeway and keep driving, never looking back at the exit you just left."

Here is a checklist that challenges you to look closely at self to determine if you not only have your walking shoes on but are ready to walk away from toxic people, places, and things that mean you harm rather than good:

1. When mediocre begins to annoy you because the desire to operate in excellence is beginning to consume your internal world. In other words, you are changing from the inside out. Your thoughts are changing, your walk is changing, you even look different,

2. When you finally wake up and smell the coffee about the fact that people are only out for what they can get from you, rather than what they can deposit into you,

3. When the places you used to go and the things you used to do are not appealing to you anymore,

4. When you have run out of excuses for why you should stay in unhealthy relationships,

5. When you realize that life is not all about you but rather it is about fulfilling purpose that will have an impact on people both near and far, and

6. When you start seeing yourself differently and refuse to let those around you devalue your self-worth.

Thought-Provoking Questions

1. Where are toxins most prevalent in your life - mind, emotions, relationships, or all three?

Thought-Provoking Questions

2. What noticeable signs confirm that you are toxic?

Thought-Provoking Questions

3. What detoxification process will you start employing in your life?

Chapter 5

SETTING BOUNDARIES AND
PERSONAL RULES FOR SELF

"The most powerful practice you can put into place to
reframe your reality is establishing healthy boundaries"
(Trimm, 2020, p.42).

As you well know, the many hats we wear as women require a lot
from us. They require our time, our personal space, our energy, our
sleep, our unselfishness, our commitment, our undivided attention,
our generosity, our patience, and the list goes on and on. It is not
that we do not love and take pride in what we do, but why does it
seem as though the opportunity to exhale and reconnect with self is
becoming few and far between? Is it because we lack clear boundaries and established rules to serve as a safeguard for preserving self?
Let me stop here for a moment and say that preserving self can take
on a plethora of meanings. However, preserving self is predicated
on establishing boundaries and reinforcing those boundaries with
"personal laws" that protect one's overall well-being. In addition,
boundaries allow you and I to reposition ourselves so that we do
not feel depleted when giving to others. The frequent burnouts, the
mental overloads, and/or the physical fatigue we are currently experiencing or have experienced could possibly be related to very
little to no limitations on how much we should give of ourselves
without first taking care of self. If you recall in Chapter 1, I indicated that recovering and maintaining self from being lost in the mix
weighs heavily on establishing boundaries that clearly differentiate

between when it is time to serve others and when it is time to attend to self. For many, there are no lucid boundaries in place to undergird their personal lives; one's authenticity of self becomes dim while the needs and/or the concerns of others become more heightened and vivid in sight. If boundaries are essential from the standpoint that they provide a standard in which respect is mutually acknowledged and acted by self and others, then rules or what I call personal laws will enforce the boundaries that are set in place to preserve self. For every boundary, there should be a rule or rules to support its existence. I will provide you an example of a rule for each boundary discussed in this chapter.

So, with that being said, let's explore what a woman with many hats looks like when boundaries are clear and personal laws are securely in place, causing her internal world to remain strong, stable, and clear as she engages with the external world. Sound familiar?

During this journey of creating a new version of you, there are three specific boundaries - mental, relational, and personal - that I consider to be game-changers for all women who are in desperate need of having a "life" balance between preserving self and serving others. Let's look closely at each of these three game changers in an effort to gain insight on how to strategically position each boundary so that we can wear our many hats graciously and not grudgingly. One caveat before we begin. As soon as you start setting boundaries and enforcing rules to protect self, do not be surprised when those who benefit from the hats you wear start experiencing withdrawal. They will be alright. Take care of yourself first so that you can take proper care of others. Let this be your motto in life.

Mental Boundary

The ability to think is something that we all should be graceful for. Because there are many facets of the mind - recalling, dreaming, imagining, analyzing, reasoning - we can easily overexert our minds to the point that they can sometimes become dull or not as sharp as usual. This overexertion keeps us from functioning at our highest level. Case in point, have you ever felt like your mind hurts just to think? LOL!! Or, if you have to think about one more thing, you are going to scream? Or have you found yourself unable to make sound decisions because you were mentally fatigued? If you answered yes to one or all of these questions, then you need to hurry up and install boundaries in your life. Two things are important here: maintaining your sanity and putting your mind on a regular rest and reset schedule so that it can effectively do what it was designed to do.

So, what does a mental boundary look like? I want you to go find a rope (nothing less than 12 inches) and lay it across your family room floor. Let one side of the rope represent your mind and the other side represent people, places, and things in your life. The rope symbolizes the boundary needed to separate the mind, which is your internal world from people, places, things, that are connected to your external world. Write down on a piece of paper something such as (habits, people, social events, and affairs of the world) that affect your thought life. Now, ask yourself the following questions: 1) How much time is allocated toward the people, places, and things in your life? Rate these time allotments on a scale of 1 to 10 with 1 meaning very little, 5 meaning somewhat, and 10 meaning total consumption. 2) Are most thoughts you have during the days about certain people, places, or things mainly positive or negative? In other words, who is renting the most space in your mind? Look at your results very carefully and then create a rule or rules that will be sturdy enough to undergird this boundary. For instance, one plan would be to make a habit of keeping your mind on positive, uplifting things, despite the negativity that tries to flow into your mind. Craft rule one by taking at least two 10-minute mental naps every day to rest and reset your mind. Shape rule two by thinking more about the solution rather than the problem. I was at Target one morning after working out at the gym. After I placed all of my must haves in the shopping basket, I decided to head towards the home decor section before leaving the store. While I was browsing, I began to engage in small-scale conversation with a store representative who was diligently organizing the shelves. In the midst of our conversation, I was explaining to her the importance of resting and resetting the mind at least twice a day so that the mind will be refreshed and alert. She laughed with a sarcastic undertone and said, "I don't have time for that!" As we departed our separate ways, I was saddened by the fact that she did not think enough of herself to at least consider the suggestion of taking time out to infuse her mind with some tender loving care and structure. A mind that is not properly tamed will evenly tame its owner.

Relational Boundary

The second boundary that I consider to be a game changer when it comes to living a balance life is relational. Relational boundaries define the amount of interaction that should be administered towards others without infringing on one's individuality. In other words, this boundary protects you from losing you. For instance, having a relational boundary between a mother and her children is vital from the standpoint that it allows the mother to interact with her children as she nurtures, guides, imparts wisdom, and loves them. However, this same boundary can become slightly rigid as the interaction between the mother and her children shifts from "we" to "me," which enables the mother to embrace her authenticity without the interruption of her children. Note: This can be a very touchy boundary when created because people, especially family members and even close friends, feel as though they have access to you 24/7. This rule will support the existence of this boundary: once the personal or professional need(s) of the person/people you are interacting with are met, then it is time to break away and reconnect or fellowship with self.

Personal Space Boundary

The third boundary that compliments a balanced life is personal space. Someone may ask, "Are the relational and personal space boundaries the same?" They are similar from the standpoint that both personal space and relational boundaries define how much of self should be given during the course of interacting with others. However, the distinction between the two is the relational boundary prevents an individual from completely surrendering self (losing self in the mix) while interacting with others, while the personal space boundary gives an individual the opportunity to take time out to pamper self through enjoying activities (i.e., spa treatments, reading a good book, going to the movies by yourself, etc.). Relational is protecting self and personal space is enjoying self.

I believe the most overlooked boundary is personal space. Women, in general, make excuses when they explain why occupying and embracing their personal space is not a priority. "My children need me!" "When I come home from work, the only thing I can think about is going to bed." "My private time went out the door when I got married and had children." The negative outcome that derives from making excuses causes women to be frustrated, overwhelmed, moody, emotionally broken, and even resentful. A simple rule to enforce is carving out quality time and participating in pleasurable activities that cause you and others to respect your personal space.

I cannot emphasize enough how mental, relational, and personal space boundaries are game-changers when it comes to living a balanced life. For it is the responsibility of every woman who wears many hats to be a good custodian over her mind, relationships, and personal time. Boundaries are not an option but a requirement for living a productive and fulfilling life. We make so many deposits into the lives of others, so it is only right that we make deposits back into ourselves.

Reflection Questions

1. Out of the three boundaries discussed in this chapter (mental, relational, and personal space), which one is the most needed in your life? Why?

Reflection Questions

2. What would be different in your life if you had boundaries in place?

Reflection Questions

3. What rules are needed to prevent you and others from crossing over the fence and violating the boundaries you have established for your life?

Chapter 6

SELECTING YOUR CIRCLE
OF INFLUENCE WISELY

Life is a sum total of whom you spend your life with.

What group of people have the most influence in your life, either personally or professionally? Briefly reflect on the people who are the closest to you. Who would you consider to be the most respectful and supportive of the many hats you wear? And who would you consider to be the least respectful? Out of all the people that you have in your circle of influence, who is faithful when it comes to depositing words of encouragement into your life? Not expecting anything in return, but genuinely wanting your hats to remain on securely while you diligently deposit into the lives of others? As we continue this journey of replenishing ourselves, I believe the content within this chapter will not only challenge you but equip you to reevaluate your current circle of influences to determine if revamping is a consideration, especially as you move to the next phase in your life. In this chapter I will address the following: 1) circles of influence and their purpose; 2) internal and external processes of connecting with people, and 3) phases affixed to circles of influence.

Circles of Influence and Their Purpose

I never want to take for granted that everyone has a lucid understanding of a circle of influence, nor do I want to assume that everyone knows the purpose behind having a stable and positive circle of influence in your life. Let's start with defining circles of influence. A circle of influence, as it relates to relationships, is being connected with people who are not only like-minded but possess the ability to reciprocate words of wisdom in addition to exemplifying an admirable lifestyle among each other, which enhances the character, actions, and overall personal growth and development of all those involved. A mouthful, right! Note: Keep in mind that a circle of influence can also have a negative connotation. Therefore, a circle of influence can also be read as such: being connected with people who are like-minded and possess the ability to reciprocate discouraging words in addition to exemplifying a deplorable lifestyle that pollutes the character, actions, and overall personal growth and development of all those involved. The purpose behind being part of a healthy circle of influence is that it breeds success, confidence, clarity of one's purpose in life, productivity, purposeful vision, people-centered leaders as opposed to self-centered leaders, accountability, creativity, self-worth, and a positive perspective in life. All of which transpires as an individual matures during this growth process. Always remember, when you know the purpose of a thing, you are less likely to abuse it.

The Internal and External Process of Connecting with People

Connecting with people is separate from being just an external process, but there is an internal process that becomes active as we begin to establish relationships outside of self. The external process is what I call the outer layer, which consists of physical interactions that transpose between two or more people, such as attending social events, communicating by phone, texting, zoom, etc. The internal process, which can also be referred to as the inner layer, is more in-depth from the standpoint that you are examining one's motives to determine if connecting with people is solely for personal gain or to be influential in the lives of all parties involved. Because association brings assimilation, an individual cannot afford to haphazardly affiliate with just anyone. However, there is a level of discernment or sensitivity a person must employ to confirm if the social, emotional, mental, moral, and social themes of an individual or group of people are a productive match. The bottom line is this: follow your heart and not your mind before allowing people access into your circle and before you enter theirs.

The Phases Within One's Circle of Influences

Whether it be initiating relationships or exiting a relationship, you will discover that your circles of influence go through phases. Many people have the preconceived notion that everything stays the same when it doesn't. Life demands change even when we are not prepared to accommodate its request. So it is, behind our own individual curtain of life we will periodically experience shifts in our circle of influences as people, including ourselves, change for whatever reason.

The phases or the shifts that occur within one's circle of influence are designed to mature, strengthen, and assist an individual in gaining a better insight on the value people (self-included) place on relationships and the roles they are expected to play. Within the bounds of each phase or shift, there are the dos, don'ts, and warning signs. These protocols and cautionary measures discussed in this chapter will assist you in effectively operating inside your circle to get the most out of impartations, mentorship, and exemplary lifestyles each member brings into the relationship.

The phases that are put into motion are the following: 1) Initial phase consists of getting acquainted with people who came across your path or vice versa either by a reputable referral and/or personal pre-destined encounter. This particular phase is what I call the "feeling each other out phase" where both parties begin to engage in social gatherings (i.e., zoom meetings, events, etc.) to determine if there is an emotional, mental, or moral social chemistry which allows either party to be possibly considered as potential candidates to join one's circle of influence.

The middle phase is what I refer to as a "settling in phase" where both parties are still learning each other, but at the same time imparting wisdom, investing one's time, sharing information, and/or mentoring. This is when relational growth is at its best as the circle becomes tighter, stronger, and more defined.

The seasonal phase is bittersweet. You will discover that some people will remain in your circle for a lifetime, but others will either dismissed themselves or you will dismiss them for various reasons. More will be discussed in the seasonal phase during the next section of this chapter, so hold on to your hat. You will notice that each phase comes in cycles as we navigate through new territory in our lives and seize new opportunities that are bestowed upon us.

Let's bring this chapter on home by exploring the cautionary measures to take as it relates to affiliating with people outside of self. These cautionary measures, these bundles of dos and don'ts are made available so you can be forewarned to avoid unnecessary disappointments and mistakes, and most importantly, to get the most out of your circles of influence.

Cautionary Measure # 1

Before Entering into The Wrong Circle

Have you ever felt a sense of unrest deep on the inside when you were in the presence of someone you met for the first time? Or have you ever decided or were about to make a decision and peace was nowhere to be found? Have you ever gone somewhere knowing good and well that you should never have stepped foot in the building? If we pull up the mental file on our past, there were always warning signs, commonly known as red flags, staring us in the face, but for some reason or another, we ignored them. Just think: those unpleasant, uncomfortable, seemingly unbearable moments in our lives could have been avoided if only we had just taken heed of the signs. Our past mistakes can either be our worst enemy or they can be our best teacher.

Since time is of the essence, beautiful ladies, we must always recruit wisdom and patience when connecting with people. No two stories are ever the same regarding how people's paths crossed, but one thing is constant, there are always signs present to apprise if one should or should not enter into a relationship.

If the circle of influence you are possibly considering connecting with is known for being self-centered, the Me, Myself and I Clique, you might want to stay clear of it. This group of people is deficient in the following areas: 1) Being sensitivity towards others and socially distance from people outside their circle. They consider themselves exclusive and only connect with people who are of the same caliber or higher. More so than not, those who only want to glean from their accomplishments are made to feel insignificant when attempting to approach them to give a compliment. As a result of this pious attitude, the opportunity to be a positive mentor or role model from afar has been forfeited, and 2) Deficiency in addressing any character flaws, insecurities, and/or fluctuating emotions that are the byproduct of failing to address the areas of brokenness in their lives. The members that makeup this circle have perfected "pretending" to the point that they have convinced themselves they are superior. Wow! For this reason alone, this group should be unappealing to you. The bottom line is this, people who are not authentic should be avoided at all costs. Ladies, wearing many hats carries its own weight, so we certainly do not need any extra luggage. If people are unable to deposit enriched substance that will assist in creating a new version of you, please leave them alone.

Cautionary Measure #2

When Not to Allow Someone in the Circle

I hope you know that everyone is not your friend. There are some people whom you should never allow to enter into your life. The instability, the brokenness, the emotional roller coaster rides, the jealousy, the hidden agendas, the power plays that are openly brought into the relationship or released in dosages during the course of the relationship makes everything complex, causing misery to outweigh pleasure. When given the opportunity to talk to someone whose relationship went sour, the main question I asked was were there any signs that forewarned them to stay clear from this person? Ninety-nine percent of the time, the answer is yes! Cautionary signs as they relate to relationships are not designed to rule over your life but are designed to protect you from harm's way, whether the signs are physical, mental, emotional, social, or moral.

There are many reasons that are worthy to be noted why one should not allow or invite someone in their circle of influence. However, I just want to briefly draw your attention to two red flags I consider to be the ultimate warning signs for tightly closing your circle when an individual possesses these traits:

1. **Knows everything and devalues the opinions of others. Do you personally know someone who thinks he/she knows everything? I do, and it can be quite annoying. A person who knows everything is no longer teachable. I believe the culprits behind an individual being convinced that she is all-knowing are:**
    a) **the fear of not being accepted by others**
    b) **childhood and/or adolescent experiences where the individual was never acknowl edged or humiliated for giving her opinion. As a result, the individual adopted a defense mechanism, devaluing the opinions of others, in order to maintain a superior position of knowing more than others.**

2. **Having priors of being an instigator. An instigator finds pleasure in starting fires by way of gossiping, lying, and/or misconstruing words of those connected to the circle, causing the relationship between the members to be fractured.**

If the instigator is not removed from the group, the authenticity of the circle loses it "innocence" to mistrust, distorting the shape of the group by turning it into a hexagon. Words of Wisdom: If you do not feel at peace about either entering someone's circle of influence or about you entering theirs, don't do it. Follow your heart!

Cautionary Measure #3

When It's Time to Exit a Circle of Influence

There are relationships that last for a lifetime, and there are others that are seasonal. Relationships that are seasonal can either be a mutual distancing with no hard feelings or they can bittersweet with a residue of resentment left behind. Seasonal relationships should not be considered as a bad thing, but should be seen as an exit in which an individual gets off because his or her purpose for being in another person's life (or vice versa) has come to a conclusion. Granted, everyone's exit moment is different, but what remains constant is the fact that there is always an inner knowing and/or an outward sign or signs preparing you for the shift that is about to transpire within your circle of influence if you pay attention. Note: Not all relationships established within your circle of influence are seasonal. There are some relationships that will last a lifetime as a result of the friendship being more in-depth as it possesses the qualities that make up an inner circle. Personally, I found myself to be at a pivotal point in my life regarding being emotionally and mentally at ease with certain relationships gradually fading into the sunset as their season came to an end. As I look back on the people who entered and exited my life, the following signs were present:

1. **Preoccupation with life. Can you think of at least one person who allows life to orchestrate their emotions and thoughts to the point that he/she alienates those around them? Leav-**

ing messages on their voicemail and sending encouraging text messages that are probably viewed but ignored are tactics used for cutting down the weeds in hopes that the beautiful flowers will bloom (friend deciding to pick up the phone or respond to texts). Once the flowers have blossomed, the aroma released from the flower is full of wisdom, laughter, and encouragement. However, once your friend retreats back into their world, preoccupied with life, the flower (the friend) withers and eventually is covered with weeds (life). Too much, right?

2. Out-of-sight, out-of-mind mentality. The physical distance between members of your circle can carry over into physical actions among those in the circle, making the commitment to remain diligent in contributing to the overall well-being of the members who are physically distant less of a priority. I was talking to close friend, and she asked me the following question, "What if it has been a long time since I have talked to a certain person, but once the two of us had the opportunity to talk, we both picked up where we left off?" I told her it would be more effective if you would periodically leave a text message to let the person know that you are thinking about them (and vice versa) rather than for them to question your intentions when you finally do call.

3. Mentally retired. When those within your circle of influence cease from seeing themselves excelling to another level but have become mentally satisfied with being at a plateau in life. What they fail to realize is one's purpose in life never ceases to end as long as one exists

here on earth. The very thought of developing new relationships can bring an uneasiness from within, but as you gently dismiss yourself in love from people whose seasons (in the capacity of a mentor) have ended, you will begin to walk into another season of your life where you will meet people who are strategically put into place to be instrumental in your growth and development as you create the new version you in order to wear your many hats in excellence.

Reflection Questions

1. What phase are you currently in - the Beginning or the Initial, Middle, or Seasonal? And what are you learning during this phase?

Reflection Questions

2. How do you determine if someone qualifies to be part of your circle of influence?

Reflection Questions

3. What cautionary measure mentioned in this chapter do you find difficult to employ in your life and why?

Chapter 7

GETTING ACQUAINTED WITH LAUGHTER

*The tightness in the stomach that aches, however
refreshing, the release of tears, the gasping for air,
the grabbing of the face, emotions exploding, it is
contagious and filling to a weary soul . . . laughter.*

When was the last time you had a good hearty laugh that had you
in tears? One of the most freeing emotions a person could experience is the emotion of laughter. I mean the type of laughter that
causes you to cringe. Laughter is the ray of sunlight of the soul and
an encouragement of tomorrow. Laughter will cause you to forget
anxieties of tomorrow and enable you to release the pressure of depression, doubt, and fear. It's freeing. It's Life. It's harmony to your
heartaches. It's peace when you want to cry. Indeed, it is medicine.
In fact, it is better than medicine . . . it's natural.

In the days we live in, many tend to get engrossed in their daily
activities and forget to laugh. Laughter is worth its weight in gold.
According to Dan Ferber (2007), laughter has the unique ability to
enhance one's intelligence, creativity, and productivity. Ladies, we
must be heedful that we do not become so consumed with all that is
entailed with wearing our many hats that we neglect to incorporate
laughter (and/or a smile) into our daily schedule. Laughter in and of
itself not only ushers in a joyful presence, but it also summons one's
inward reality - mind, will, and emotions - to arise to the occasion
when it seems as though fulfilling the demands of those around you

are overwhelming. I hope this chapter finds you well - body, soul, and mind - as you get acquainted with laughter. Laughter is like medicine for all those who choose to laugh (Ferber, 2007).

The Benefits of Laughter

Laughter the Buffer

Laughter is a buffer which shields you from the emotional and mental cuts and bruises that result from worry, fear of the unknown, stress, inadequacies, and/or a sense of helplessness that either oozes from random thoughts painted on the canvas of one's imagination, and/ or a high alert of one's negative emotions as you attempt to make sense of life's challenges. When an individual employs laughter, it immediately intervenes by becoming the sword that pierces through the thickness of the problem so that an individual can get a glimpse of the sunlight, causing her to press through the situation so that she can rise to a new level of strength with a greater capacity to do what she was called to do in life. Even though wearing many hats can draw conflicts, involuntary changes, and/or challenges, laughter will assist you in making life rather than life making you.

Laughter Is a Life Vest

Life has its up and downs, highs and lows, setbacks, triumphs, twists, and turns. You never know what hand life will deal you, but rest assured, laughter saves. Laughter is like a lifeguard throwing a life vest out to sea in order that the individual will not sink. The vest of laughter is your declaration that you will not surrender your peace in the midst of stressful situations. I just chuckled at the times when I thought of quitting but laughter, my life vest, would not let me because it gripped me tight. Its adjustable clasps secured me to a safe place. Laughter will keep you afloat even when it feels like you are drowning in a sea of insurmountable responsibilities, obligations, and/or the weight of those around you pulling you in every direction. Laughter is drawn from the many veins from which humor can be found. Whether it be from a comedian within the family, a friend, or a good movie, laughter has the ability to turn your emotions and thoughts in the right direction, from negative to positive. Additionally, laughter, the life vest, creates a weather resistance environment which prevents the negativity associated with the storms of life from seeping through and disturbing your inner reality. Laughter encases your internal world with hope, reassurance, and a sense of ease so that you can successfully overcome life's challenges and move on, stronger and better.

Laughter Cleanses

Finally, laughter is refreshing because it cleanses or remove the debris left behind from stress, worry, fear, and depression. To laugh helps detox our minds by removing the negativity which not only puts limitations on our ability to enjoy life to the fullest, but also interferes with our ability to give our all to those who benefit from the many hats we wear. Just think how refreshed and relaxed you felt after taking a bath or shower. Well, the same refreshing and relaxing experience takes place during a good hearty laugh. This therapeutic remedy, better known as laughter, soothes your mind, emotions, and physical body while being lathered with the feel-good neurotransmitter, dopamine, which stimulates the frontal lobe of the brain (Ferber, 2007).

Who Makes You Laugh?

Having the right people in your life means everything. Each person plays a vital role in your life that makes the journey more meaningful. You may have friends and/or relatives whose roles may vary from being a good listener, counselor, encourager, and even a mentor, but one should never, never, never be without someone who has the ability to make him or her laugh. I once heard someone say that everyone needs at least one person in their life who has the sole responsibility of making them laugh. In other words, this individual (or individuals) through his or her humorous disposition has the ability to usher laughter into the atmosphere to bring relief to those who suffer from emotional and mental fragility. Often, this frailness is the byproduct of being too consumed with life so that living a balanced life is not an option. This specific friend and/or family member carries the mantle of laughter, which brings tightness in the stomach that aches, causes tears to stream down your face, makes you gasp for air, and even causes you to grab your face.

So go call your friend, that designated family member, and get your laugh on. Treat yourself to a good laugh; it will be one of the best deposits you ever made in your life. Laughter is contagiously healthy for those who dare to draw from its uplifting power. Let's continue with our journey as we learn how to pursue peace!

Reflection

1. Describe how you incorporate laughter in your life.

Reflection

2. Describe a time when laughter became your life vest, buffer, or both.

Chapter 8

DEFENDING YOUR PEACE

Peace needed the most but the least sought after. While peace is known to have excellent health benefits, people still choose stress and its detrimental effects rather than be at ease. Peace is priceless, but some would rather settle for something of little or no value. Peace is a gift that is often unwrapped. Peace is a shield, but some rather go unprotected. I wrote this particular chapter from a position of a warrior fighting in battle defending what he or she holds to be true or of value. As women, we are constantly combatting life challenges, shame, guilt, toxic relationships, fear, insecurities, brokenness, and the memories of past mistakes that try to arise against our peace and ambush our thoughts and emotions until they are held captive, IF YOU LET THEM! Nothing or no one can disturb your peace without you giving it or someone permission. Without further ado, let's continue our journey as we explore the essence of peace, the various capacities that peace serves, and finally, how to protect one's peace. Enjoy the journey as we travel down the road called peace.

The Essence of Peace

I cannot reiterate enough how the lack of understanding the purpose of a thing will cause its existence to be mishandled. However, once clarity has been gained, it allows the individual to receive what the person and/or thing has to offer. Then, the person can appropriate the item accordingly. During the course of learning about a person or thing, the nature and attributes of the thing (or person) begin to unfold as they become reality in one's life, defining what is and what is not.

So it is, the essence of peace is quite distinct and cannot be compared to any other. If it sounds like I am referring to peace as a person, I am! I want you to begin visualizing peace as your best friend, as a noun. A best friend who has your best interest at heart and is therefore well deserving of being respected, appreciated, and highly valued in your life, especially during those times when confusion is swirling all around you. If you stay connected to peace, familiarizing yourself with the nature of peace, you will begin to recognize when peace is present and when peace has been overshadowed by external distractions (i.e., relational discord, financial hardship, challenges in the workplace, health issues, etc.) which are flavored with distasteful condiments such as fear, frustration, anxiety, uncertainties, etc. That's why I make every effort to always lock arms with my best friend. Not just during those unexpected turbulent moments in my life, but also during those calm, "all is well" moments. You may say, "Sheryl, how do I lock arms with peace?" You accomplish this by thinking positive thoughts and saying uplifting words that send an invitation to peace to come in, consume your mind, and settle your emotions. However, if the theme of your life is centered around being stressed out and the majority of your thoughts and words are filled with doom and gloom, then peace will never be an option for you. Peace is always accessible, but it must be a desired state of being.

Here is what I have found to be true regarding the nature of peace:

1. **Peace is consistent. Peace remains steady, forever unchanging even during good times and not so good times. Peace is always present even when I fail to acknowledge my best friend's presence.**

2. **Peace is gentle.** The calming nature of peace resonates throughout my internal world, allowing me to enjoy life, to make clear decisions, and to overcome rather than surrender to adversities in life.

3. **Peace does not compromise.** Peace does not have to settle or alter its nature because peace is constant. Peace is an absolute state of being that is not dependent on one's conditional state (i.e., economic status, social status, etc.), but peace is an inward knowing, an unexplainable assurance that things are going to change for the better even when one's physical senses say otherwise, and

4. **Peace is not competitive.** Peace is readily attainable and faithful to those who choose to embrace its presence. However, one thing peace will not do is compete for your attention, especially when you mingle with negative thoughts that endlessly serenade you with hopelessness regarding the situation at hand.

Peace Is A(n) . . .

Umpire

A plump juicy kosher hotdog cuddled between a warm soft bun, generously covered with ketchup, mustard, or both. Buttery, salted popcorn accompanied by an ice-cold beverage. The laughter, non-sport-related chitter-chatter and the resounding cheers resonating throughout the stadium as family and friends enjoy fellowship with each other while watching the game. A crowd standing anxiously awaiting as an umpire calls out, "Safe!!!!!!," while the player takes a dive and stretches out his hands, touching home base. Peace is an umpire that will warn you if either a business adventure, a relationship, purchasing a new home, a decision related to your family, a career change, and let's not forget taking on a new hat, is safe or not. When you become acquainted with peace, when you stay in fellowship with peace, you will find it easier to distinguish between the uneasiness on the inside ("not safe") as opposed to the assurance, the confidence, the ease that takes root within your inner world that confirms that peace is on the scene and has made the official call, "Safe."

Protector

Peace is a protector. When your internal reality has truly embraced the presence of peace, peace takes on the role of a protector. Meaning, peace begins to cover or shield you from the side effects (I.e., stress, worry, fear) that are the byproduct of outside elements - demands of life, challenges, negativity, uncertainties, etc., that try to pressure you to respond outside the domain of peace. In other words, peace protects you so that you will not be seduced to give up, cave in, or throw in the towel. Peace, your best friend, covers you so that your internal reality remains strong, stable, and lucid. Peace keeps your internal reality from beginning to resemble the obstacles of life (external reality).

How to Keep Your Peace

It takes effort to maintain anything or anyone worth keeping in your life. Ladies, for all the hats we will wear in our lifetimes, it is a must to have and maintain a solid relationship with peace. If you have ever had a relationship with stress, shame, guilt, depression, or fear, you can surely take time to establish a relationship with peace. I make it a habit to do the following to solidify my relationship with peace: 1) Monitoring what I allow to enter into my eye gate and ear gate, 2) Speaking positive words into my life that acknowledge the presence of peace, 3) Tenaciously holding on to my peace regardless of what is going on around me, 4) Respectfully trusting in the guidance of peace as a I navigate through life, 5) Being selective in who I allow to enter into my world. The wrong people in your life will not only steal your peace but your joy, if you let them, 6) Living from the inside out and not from the outside in, 7) Spending time alone with self heightens my sensitivity to the realness of peace in my life, 8) Quickly eradicating thoughts that try to challenge my peace. I have found if I ponder long enough on negative or unrealistic thoughts, I begin to drift away from my peace, and 9) Reminding myself that peace is not an outward appearance and/or accumulation of things acquired in life but an inward knowing. A person could know about eruptions in the world but still have peace.

Beautiful ladies, don't allow being at peace to be just a hit and miss experience in your life, but rather make it a habit to live in peace. Start seeing peace as your best friend, not an abstract concept. Be diligent in cultivating your relationships by spending time with peace in order to not only understand but appreciate the nature of peace. To love peace is to know peace. Finally, all that we must do as women, whether we feel like it or not, is allow peace to be your umpire and your protector as you walk down this path called life. PEACE!!!!

Questions

1. If peace was truly your best friend, what things in your life would you cease from worrying about?

Questions

2. Is peace your umpire, protector, or both? Why?

Questions

3. Describe a moment in your life when you were at peace.

Chapter 9

GOOD RIDDANCE OFFENSIVENESS

Every time you get offended, you experience a stop
and pause moment in your life which interferes
with your effectively living from the inside out
as opposed to the outside in.

The next two chapters are going to require you to remove things in your life that are taking up space in your mind and resurfacing negative emotions. Although this journey we are on is primarily about depositing back into self, we must add another factor into this equation, and that is our willingness to being open to getting rid of excess baggage - passive thoughts, emotional security blankets, hurt and pain, disappointments, offenses, and intolerance - that has been hoarding in our lives for a long time. Ladies, no longer will we allow unforgiveness and offensiveness to be our traveling companions as we journey through life.

Cindy Trimm, a profound teacher, said, "Most people cannot embrace their amazing future because they refuse to let go of the baggage they're carting." (2020, p.51-52). People are subconsciously hoarding their pasts with the preconceived notion that one day they might need to reach back into their arsenal and pull up something in their past in order to address their present situation. As a result, their negative actions and/or reactions have not only justified why they are the way they are, but also, these actions and reactions have become their crutches in life. Regardless of the number of hats you wear in life, you will never fully operate in your role as a mother, businesswoman, educator, etc., until you can let go of the excess luggage. There is no doubt you are a good mother, teacher, etc., but are you operating in excellence? Are you fully capable of releasing your fullest potential? What are you hoarding in your life that is robbing you from operating in a place of excellence? There are two luggage brands that I will be showcasing during the next two chapters, offensiveness and unforgiveness. Let's start with luggage number one, Offensiveness. Offensiveness is when someone feels intensely hurt or damaged, insulted, upset and/or angered that he or she has been offended, permitting distasteful moments (i.e., being intentionally attacked or being overly sensitive). The offended person's internal reality begins to dictate how they respond to their external reality. If not properly treated, offensiveness, like a potter, begins to mold and shape one's hurt, pain, anger, bitterness, and resentment into unforgiveness. Many of you out there have been offended to the extent that you are unable to trust others. As a result, you have either consciously or unconsciously encapsulated yourself within your internal world to the point that your contact with others is far and few between. Both mentally and emotionally, you put a lid on, paralyzed, entrapped in your ability to share your gifts, talents, contributions, and potential by way of your external reality (life) through the many hats you wear. In other words, you can only see you, and nothing or no one else matters. So, let's roll up our sleeves and start unpacking any and everything that resembles offensiveness in our lives so that we can move to a better place.

What Does It Mean To Be Offended?

To make sure you and I are on the same page, what does it actually mean to be offended? To be offended is when someone feels immensely hurt or damaged, insulted, disrespected, or upset as a result of one's character, suggestions offered, professional performance, beliefs, and/or identity being negatively attacked or downplayed by others through their action or words. Being offended is by choice, not by force. In other words, no one has the power to cause you to be offended, but rather it is a mental and emotional consent given by you, which allows the impact of the words or actions (either directly or indirectly) to enter into your internal reality and cause a disturbance. If not dealt with immediately, offensiveness will eventually take root in your internal reality, causing the following to occur: 1) Inability to concentrate on what you are called to do as a result of the feelings of hurt that are constantly bombarding your thoughts as you replay the situation over and over again; 2) Hesitation to serve or give of self fully for the fear of being hurt; 3) Confinement to a "woe is me" mentality, which disables you from looking beyond self; 4) Interference with your ability to walk in the boldness and confidence needed when overseeing and imparting into the lives of those connected to the many hats you wear; and 5) Minimization of your ability to discern when others are for you as opposed to being against you.

Types of Offense

Everyone has the opportunity to be offended, but not everyone will engage in the moment. To label or classify offensiveness as being the same for everyone is wrong. Why? No two people are the same, and every situation is different. The difference between someone either consenting to or resisting offensiveness is predicated on if the comment and/or action directed towards a person is worth acknowledging. In other words, is it worth exerting time and energy (both emotionally and mentally) towards something that adds no value to who you are?

There are primarily two ways in which an individual displays his or her offensiveness: silently or openly. Silent offense is when the individual internalizes the words or actions connected to the situation and begins to mentally rehearse the event over and over again. As a result, not only is there a mental reoccurrence of the event, but there is also a rewritten version, including what could have been done differently. This replay of the event allows the individual to mentally seek revenge as she undoes the original scene by imagining herself responding differently to the situation, therefore having the advantage. An individual who has internalized offensiveness usually displays the following outward behavior patterns:

1. **Very little to no communication with the person who offended them.**

2. **Makes it a point to keep one's distance - socially, physically, and emotionally towards the person who offended them.**

3. **Periodically relives the event by sharing it with others, seeking validation for feelings surrounding the situation at hand.**

The second type of offense is what I call **Openly Displayed Offensivenes**. This is when an individual openly unveils the hurt, the displeasure directed towards him or her either through words and/or actions. By publicly retaliating, the person conveys a message that one's internal reality (which houses one's belief system, identity, emotions, etc.) is unsettled, disturbed, and angry. Therefore, by outwardly expressing hurt, either verbally or physically, the person not only justifies his or her actions but also provides a sense of gratification, both mentally and emotionally.

Those who publicly display offense often revisit the event by telling those who will listen in hopes of receiving sympathy and recruiting supporters. Those who join the bandwagon personally take on the individual's hurt and resentment as if they actual experience the event themselves. They have bitten into this forbidden fruit, causing seeds to spread and eventually take root in their internal reality. This bitterness creates a tree that produces the fruit called offensiveness.

Rising above Offensiveness

As I indicated earlier, everyone has had the opportunity to be offended, but not everyone will engage in the moment. What causes some people to become easily offended while others let things roll off them like water rolls off a duck's back? I believe it is how a person positions herself that will determine how often she will take advantage of the opportunity to get offended. Someone who is always subject to being upset, angered, or humiliated as a result of what was said or done will always be held in bondage to people rather than being free from people. So how do we as women, whose makeup is normally more sensitive than our counterparts, rise above situations where words, thoughts, and actions have the ability to rub against our internal reality the wrong way? How do we arise above offensiveness?

1. **Condition your mind to think and exercise your mouth to speaking words that confirm or seal in what is true about who you are (your identity), what you are capable of doing (your talents or gifts) and what you are capable of having in life. In other words, solidify your existence here on this earth through words, which help manage or keep your thoughts and emotions anchored when you are tempted to be offended.**

2. **Be quick to listen, slow to speak, and slow to respond to words and/or actions that may rub you the wrong way. Analyze what is being said or done in an effort to determine if it is beneficial or detrimental. If what is being said or done is beneficial, then see how it can be applied to your life. However, if what is being said or done is detrimental, give it no space in your mind and move on. Your first "response" (Say, "First response!") will not only determine the outcome of the situation but will also determine how long you will concentrate on the situation.**

3. **Develop tough skin. Make it point not to be so sensitive about everything. Keep in mind that there will always be something or someone (i.e., subject matters on the news, your boss, your neighbor, your spouse, colleagues, coworkers, etc.) that may intentionally or unintentionally rattle your internal reality - your belief system, your emotions, your inner image. However, as long as you are not held captive to or dictated by your external reality, you begin to have less "stop and pause" moments in your life, which can interfere with your effectively living from the inside out as opposed to the outside in. The bottom line is this: refuse to give anyone authority over your internal world. Repeat after me: "I refuse to give anyone authority over my internal world." Write this down and post this on your refrigerator or bathroom mirror: People's words cannot define your destiny unless they become part of your vocabulary.**

Overcoming being easily offended does not manifest itself overnight, so don't get frustrated. It is a growth process that occurs overtime. Not only should you acknowledge that there may be a deeply rooted tree on the inside of you, but uprooting this tree out of your life is the first step in the right direction. It is within this maturation process that one begins to reflect on self and make the necessary changes needed in order for the new version of you to accentuate the many hats you wear in life.

Reflection Questions

1. When was the last time you were offended, and how did you handle the situation?

Reflection Questions

2. What are you hoarding in your life that is robbing you from operating in a place of excellence?

Reflection Questions

3. Do you internalize offensiveness or publicly display offensiveness? Explain.

Chapter 10

THE LUGGAGE OF UNFORGIVENESS

Am I the only one who owns luggage that always feels heavy even when there is a minimal amount of apparel and accessories packed on the inside? Of course not! There are many women who are attracted, just like me, by the appearance of luggage that is naturally heavy. Even now, there is name-brand luggage that seems to hold the attention of women of all walks of life. This particular luggage is neither tangible nor attractive like many other luggage we have or want, but it can be just as heavy or even heavier than the luggage we physically carry during our travel adventures. The luggage I am referring to is unforgiveness. Unforgiveness is one of the heftiest suitcases any human being could every carry in their lifetime. Why? There are so many compartments that are stuffed with unpacked items, such as past hurts, past abuse, shame, guilt, and/or disappointments, all of which weigh heavily on one's mental, emotional, and even physical well-being, dictating how one thinks, feels, and responds to life at any given time. I know people today who appear as though they have it all together – they are physically attractive, they have a smile that can brighten a room, they have a successful career and the perfect family. However, during those quiet moments, deep within their internal reality, the luggage of unforgiveness, which has been so neatly tucked away, occasionally reopens itself and begins to agitate their thoughts and emotions as they relive the past. You see, the influence of unforgiveness is so strong that it can numb a person's will to forgive oneself and others.

The bottom line is this: people have given unforgiveness authorization to alter their demeanor and focus. Every time, they stop and watch a reenactment of past insult being displayed through the window of their mind. I have personally witnessed people who went from Dr. Jekyll to Mr. Hyde in a matter of minutes just from the mention of someone's name who was connected to the feelings, emotions, and thoughts affixed to either the betrayal, the disappointment, the malicious acts, and/or the hurtful words of the past. This chapter, along with chapter 9, "Good Riddance, Offensiveness" are what I call the "deep" cleansing of one's internal reality. Why? Both unforgiveness and offensiveness create a lot of debris that consume one's internal world. So, let's get started cleaning house by addressing the following: 1) What is unforgiveness? 2) Recognizing when unforgiveness is setting up camp in one's life; and 3) How to be released from the shackles of unforgiveness. This chapter is in no way trying to dilute the validity behind the abuse, the hurt, betrayal, guilt, or disappointment you experienced in life; rather, it is intended to assist you in obtaining emotional and mental freedom from the torment caused by the inability or unwillingness to forgive, so that you can be in the position to effectively deposit into the lives of those who draw from the many hats you wear.

What is Unforgiveness?

Unforgiveness is being unwilling, unable, stubborn, or resistant to releasing someone or self from a past experience that involves betrayal, abuse, humiliation, disappointment. and/or exploitation. Unforgiveness causes deep emotional agony and/or distrust, which dictates how one functions in life. Unforgiveness breeds bitterness and resentment, which sways one to nurture, both mentally and emotionally, hurt, distrust, and betrayal internally before externally announcing one's pain through his or her outward actions (i.e., social Isolation, etc.).

Degrees of Unforgiveness

You cannot place unforgiveness in one pot and assume everyone is going to consume the same amount. Meaning, the general definition for unforgiveness does not change, but how people interpret, internalize, and exhibit unforgiveness is different. In other words, the portrait of unforgiveness for one person's life is dissimilar to another. I would like to take it further by saying there are even degrees or levels of unforgiveness that manifest either mentally, emotionally, physically, socially, and behaviorally in the lives of those who refuse or find it difficult to disconnect from the anger and pain that stem from unforgiveness. The degrees or levels of unforgiveness are as following:

Brief episode. A short-lived mental reenactment of the event which contributes to the pain, feelings of betrayal, humiliation, and/or disappointment that harbor in one's internal reality. This portrait of unforgiveness is often put on display during the course of a casual conversation. Someone reminds you of a person who hurt you in the past, acknowledging a specific date or time of the year connected to the negative experience, or an out-of-the-blue passive thought causes a person to pause and reflect on the past. Hence, not only is one's demeanor rerouted to the former instance where it emulates the distasteful moments of the past, but it also detracts one's ability to focus on the here and now. Once the brief episode has subsided, the emotions and thoughts realign themselves with the present until one's portrait of unforgiveness resurfaces at another time.

Revolving Episodes. Occur when an individual is so engrossed, so encapsulated in her portrait of unforgiveness that she becomes trapped in the revolving door of her past. Her overall well-being (i.e., relationships, decisions, life in general) is solely predicated on the hurt, betrayal, humiliation, and distrust that constantly resurrects the past. This never-ending cycle of unforgiveness not only overshadows but also minimizes her ability to effectively function in the present. In other words, the individual lives her life through unforgiveness.

Blended Episodes. The combination of the two, brief and revolving episodes.

This portrait of unforgiveness may start off small, 5 by 7, but as the remnants of the past linger longer than usual, they begin to consume one's thoughts and emotions to the point that the portrait enlarges to an 11 by 14. As a result, pressure is placed on one's actions to relive the past, either through socially distancing oneself, blaming self, crying, using harsh words, and/or Indulging in addictive behaviors to soothe the pain. Once the individual finally regains control of his or thoughts and emotions, once the strong emotional and mental grip has subsided, the revolving door comes to a halt, the individual gets off, and the enlarged portrait begins to minimize in size and life for the individual returns to his or her present state.

Has Unforgiveness Set Up Camp in Your Life?

The phrases or lines that I hear time after time are, "I am not holding anything against her," or, "I am not walking in unforgiveness." "I released him a long time ago." All the while, their body language, their facial expressions, and their tone of voice says otherwise. You see ladies, if we are going to wear our many hats authentically, effectively, and confidently, we must be willing to search deep within to see if we are being weighed down by even the smallest luggage called unforgiveness. There is nothing more miserable than carrying a piece of luggage around that serves no purpose, luggage that is incapable of providing the essential things we need to remain focused and productive as we travel down this road called life. So, with that being said, the question that I would like to ask is how does one know if unforgiveness has set up camp in her life?

1. **Just the mention of a person, place or thing almost immediately makes an individual disconnect (emotionally and mentally) from the here and now**

and connect with past.

2. When unforgiveness becomes a crutch for why an individual is unable to move forward in life.

3. When you make innocent bystanders, such as family members and friends, suffer through your actions or words for something they had no part in.

4. Rehearsing past hurt, betrayal, humiliation, shame, and guilt as if it just happened.

5. When you find it difficult to forgive yourself for something you did in the past.

6. When you are constantly thinking of ways to seek revenge for someone who hurt you in the past.

7. Physical and mental ailments (headaches, depression, anxiety, high blood pressure, etc.) manifest in one's body as a result of internally harboring unforgiveness.

8. Distancing yourself from everyone for fear of being hurt again.

9. Finding it hard to trust anyone.

10. Justifying unforgiveness as a reasonable punishment for the pain, betrayal, humiliation, shame and/or guilt inflicted by self and/or others.

11. When peace is nonexistent in an individual's life as a result of unforgiveness having dominion over one's internal reality.

How Do I Forgive?

When you finally come to the conclusion that there is more to you than your past, you are becoming more open to forgive. When you begin to yearn for mental, emotional, and physical freedom from the internal misery caused by the unforgiveness which has held you in bondage for years, you are becoming more open to forgive. When you are sick and tired of being sick and tired of looking through the rearview mirror of your past, you are becoming more open to forgive. When you finally see unforgiveness as a liability rather than an asset in your life, you are becoming more open to forgive. When you finally decide it is time to release yourself and/or others, you are becoming more open to forgive. The healing process that is extracted from forgiveness is set into motion once the act of one's will becomes open to either reconciling with self and/or releasing others. However, this healing process is just that - a process; and therefore, involves you cleaning the hard drive of your mind that has been bombarded with the downloads of the past. I recommend the following:

1. **Acknowledging there is the luggage of unforgiveness in your life either towards self or others. Acknowledging there is unforgiveness in your life is the first step towards healing. I like to say that you can never experience true healing unless you admit that you need to be healed.**

2. **Making a quality decision to forgive and move on. Letting go of one's past can be the most difficult thing to do for the simple fact that this is where an individual's hurt, pain, feelings of betrayal, shame, guilt, and humiliation are supported the most.**

3. **Confront and eradicate thoughts which stimulate the negative emotions that undergird unforgiveness with positive words or statements (i.e., "I**

will not let my past determine my destiny," "I choose to be free," "I refuse to allow the memory of my past to hurt me anymore," etc.).

4. Make it a practice to refrain from looking through the rearview mirror where your past resides and start looking ahead where your destiny awaits.

5. Seek professional counseling.

6. Refuse to allow others to bring up the event and/ or the person attached to the hurt, feelings of betrayal, shame, guilt, etc. The goal is to release the past and not to stay in a relationship with the past.

7. Do not ponder or rehearse the past. It does not promote your future.

Truly Forgiven

So how does one know that she has truly forgiven? Let's customize this question just for you. How will you know when you have truly forgiven self and/or others? Drum roll please! The answer is, when you can release yourself and others and move on with your life. When the pain caused by being deeply pierced in the heart as a result of the betrayal, humiliation, distrust has subsided, you have truly forgiven and moved on. When the uncontrollable flow of tears has finally come to a halt, you have truly forgiven and moved on. When you no longer have to cry yourself to sleep, you have truly forgiven and have moved on. When the reenactment of the past is no longer a box office hit in your mind, you have truly forgiven and moved on.

The umbilical cord connected to your past has been cut once and for all; therefore, you can connect to your present and undauntedly pursue your destiny, which dwells in the future. Why? You have come to the conclusion that the person who hurt you is not worthy enough for you to hate nor noteworthy to be transported into your future both mentally and emotionally. The bottom line is this: the new portrait that you have created in the canvas of your imagination is bright and promising. Therefore, there is no space available for any sketches that resemble any form of unforgiveness. Imagine a caterpillar that is no longer contained in its cocoon, but has transformed into a beautiful butterfly eloquently waltzing with nature while being serenaded by his or her surroundings. Well, imagine yourself no longer held captive to your past but at liberty to not only appreciate but luxuriate while being serenaded by laughter, smiles, peace, self-love, and the love from others that exists in the here and now.

Finally, beautiful ladies, let me leave you with this. There are more pages to our lives to be read than just our past. The prior chapters in our lives, such as hurt, pain, shame, guilty, betrayal, abuse, rejection, and distrust are non-fiction, but they are not our conclusion. Refuse to allow unforgiveness to be the coauthor of your life. Put this oversized, outdated luggage to rest so that you can write the remaining chapters of your life in peace. You are free, my beautiful sisters. You are no longer held captive to the torment of unforgiveness. Tell unforgiveness it is over!! It has been talking to you for years. Now tell it to hush and listen to what you have to say. It is over!!!!! The mental and emotional affair you had with unforgiveness is over. No more succumbing to the late-night temptations to mentally romance and emotionally caress the pain, the hurt, and the shame of your past. Choose to receive the gift of letting go. The new version of you cannot fit into your past. So, walk in the freedom, the peace, and the newness of life as we continue on our journey called life.

Thought-Provoking Questions

1. What are you unwilling to let go of and why?

Thought-Provoking Questions

2. What degree of unforgiveness - Brief, Revolving, or Blended best describes your experience within unforgiveness? Explain.

Chapter 11

THE MIDST OF A CHALLENGE

It is what you do in the middle of the storm that will determine how you will come out at the end.

Is it just me or does it seem like it is difficult for those who are constantly withdrawing from the many hats we wear to conceptualize the fact that we are humans too? We have to deal with the complexities of life just like they do. We get tired just like they do. We get upset just like they do. We experience physical challenges in our bodies just like they do. Let me put my feet on the brakes right here! Why is it that ladies, especially those who occupy the role of a mother and/or wife, when we are physically tired or ill, we are still expected to prepare the meals for the family, clean the house, pick up the kids from school, have favorite snacks in the pantry, spend time with the hubby, go to work, etc., when we should be in the bed resting? I am just saying!!! It seems like the entire family goes in a "I don't know what to do" mode when we decide to attend to self. Dad, children, and even the dog, sit on the edge of the bed looking sad but concerned. Why? Because we are the HEARTBEAT of our family. Repeat after me, "I am the heartbeat of my family."

When you and I, the heartbeat of the family, slow down, the rhythmic flow of the family is placed paused. Interaction patterns customized to our families' specific daily routines are interrupted. We are so accustomed to serving everyone while on autopilot mode that when we are finally forced to land in order to take care of ourselves (when our bodies say enough!), it not only interrupts the rhythm in which we serve others, but it also disrupts the rhythm and cadence of those who are the recipients of our services. The hats you wear in life require you to have a rhythm which allows you to nurture, serve, support, impart, lead, and instruct. In other words, this rhythmic flow assists you in navigating life during the transitions that occur as you endlessly change hats to meet the demands of those being served. But what happens when a tsunami, a challenge, unexpectedly lands in your life and shatters your emotions, floods your thoughts with negativity, and enfeebles your abilities to keep your head above water, life? Do you set aside your hat or hats until the challenge has subsided? Who will attend to the needs of those who withdraw from the many hats you wear?

Come closer and absorb what I am about to say. If something happens to you, people and life will go on, so take care of yourself. This statement ("Life goes on!") became a reality to me when a tsunami in the form of severe illness attacked my body. My life had come to a screeching halt both personally and professionally; as a result, my sole focus was on living and not dying, and everything else was placed on the back burner. Thank God I am here today!!! Beautiful ladies, let's be real. We all have had tsunamis unexpectedly land in our lives. As a matter of fact, some of you are facing a tsunami while reading this book. You may not be certain if you are coming or going. You may be even contemplating throwing in the towel, BUT the fighter on the inside of you is saying just one more round. Allow me to be a messenger of glad tidings: there is a BUT after each challenge you will face in life. It just requires you to be focused, consistent, determined, and confident during the process of obtaining what rightfully belongs to you - good health, peace, healthy relationships, promotion etc. In chapters 11 and 12, I will share with you the steps I employ to overcome rather than succumb to life's challenges. Each step is specifically designed to provide: 1) mental clarity and emotional stability, 2) strength to move forward rather than remaining stuck, and 3) courage for you to stand toe to toe with a challenge, a tsunami, instead of being intimidated. Now, beautiful ladies, let's get to work with the intent to pursue what's on the other side of the But!!!!! The new version of you.

Step 1: First Response.

When a tsunami is about to land or has actually landed in your life, what is your initial response? Do your run for dear life? Do you hide in fear? Do you automatically surrender with words of defeat, drowning out all possibilities to withstand the challenge? Or, do you collect your thoughts, take a deep breath, take on the posture of a warrior - shoulder back, chest out, head up and say, "This too shall pass!" You see, what you say, how you think, and how you respond during the onset of the challenge will determine if you are going to surrender or resist. Your mental disposition, to either surrender or to resist, stems from your belief system, developed by way of repetitious information, past experience, and/or experiences of oth ers. What you hold to be true (belief system) is then communicated outwardly through your words and/or actions while addressing life issues, sculpturing the following: 1) your attitude, 2) your perception of self against the challenge, 3) your level of endurance, 4) your point of focus (on the problem or on the solution), and 5) your level of discernment when navigating through the obstacle course connected to the challenge at hand. The bottom line is this, your initial reaction towards a challenge creates a mental image which becomes the blueprint that will either lead you to victory or defeat.

Step 2: The Attitude.

Attitudes come in all different flavors: nice-nasty, positive, and negative. The flavor and attitude we choose to escort us through life become the lens we use to interpret the world in which we live in. In addition, our attitude strongly influences how we interact with people, how we respond to life experiences, and what we will accept in life.

No one is exempt from challenges. Challenges are inevitable, but they are not impossible to overcome. Your attitude at the beginning, in the middle, and at the end of challenges not only stabilizes your position (resists or defeats) but determines how you will strategically navigate through the storms of life.

If I could have you employ the canvas of your imagination for a moment, I want you to envision yourself as a passenger on a Boeing 747 that has just been cleared for departure. As the plane begins to ascend into the sky, it squeezes its way through the clusters of fluffy clouds until it reaches a cruising altitude of 36,000 for the duration of the ride. As you recline in your seat and begin to drift off to sleep, you are awakened by a forceful jerk that causes both you and the rest of the passengers to become startled. A deep voice comes over the intercom, saying, "This is your captain. We are experiencing some turbulence. Make sure you remain in your seat and fasten your seat belt. Flight attendants, please discontinue serving drinks and those iconic plane snacks, Biscoff cookies, until further notice." As the captain strategically navigates the highways of the air, you can feel the plane gradually changing altitude in an effort to minimize the turbulence or avoid it altogether. Just as the captain daringly maneuvered the Boeing 747 while dodging the unsteady movements in the air, you must strategically maneuver around the unexpected air pockets and fierce winds of life in order to land safely and proceed forward.

One's attitude becomes the interpreter for his or her belief system, either through words or actions. The attitude retrieves information from the belief system, determining one's altitude by instructing an individual to rise above the situation (both mentally and emotionally) or remain as is.

Now, write down your refusal statements. For example, "I REFUSE TO FEAR." This statement, "I refuse to fear," represents one's attitude through words. It expresses what an individual will or won't do while combatting the challenge at hand. During the pandemic, my friend and brother Carl Trent who resides in California, called me early in the morning and said, "I refuse to allow this pandemic to dictate how I smile and care for people. I will wear my mask and practice social distancing, but I refuse to allow the pandemic to dictate how I share the innate gifts on the inside of me with those near and abroad." This was Carl Trent's attitude, which determined his altitude during this world crisis.

Step 3: Reference List.

Have you ever felt all alone during a challenge? Family and friends can be all around you, but their voices are on mute as you are encapsulated in your reality where fear, uncertainties, anxiety, pain, and hurt are trying to torment your mind, emotions, and body. People are going on with their lives, the sun is rising and setting, the birds are harmoniously chirping as they are greeting a new day, while your life is seemingly at a standstill. You are exhausted and are desperately in need of a life vest just to stay afloat, while wanting to throw in the towel. Often, contemplating on caving and giving up, SOMETHING deep on the inside of you refuses to give the challenge the satisfaction of defeating you.

Even though life challenges may be individually encased with your name exclusively inscribed outside of each wrapper, tests were not designed for you to go through alone. Let me reiterate the last part of this phrase, tests were not designed for you to go through alone. I strongly believe that people are strategically and non-coincidentally placed in our lives either to assist, comfort, and/or encourage us during those personalized tsunami experiences that are unbearable at times. In the aftermath of the horrific 2004 Indian Ocean earthquake and tsunami, an estimated of 227,898 lives in 14 countries were mercilessly taken, causing it to be classified as one of the deadliest natural catastrophes in recorded history ("2004 Indian Ocean," 2022). These two elements of nature intertwined, causing an impact that harshly echoed as far as Alaska by triggering an earthquake ("2004 Indian Ocean," 2022). Here is my point: the people who survived this calamitous event were facing a humongous challenge. They were desperately in need of a reference list of people who could provide, without delay, assistance, comfort, encouragement, and guidance both with short term (food, water, shelter, etc.) and long-term support. As a result, organizations like UNICEF and the American Red Cross contributed humanitarian relief while monetary donations poured in from both the private and public sectors in the largest-ever relief response from across five countries simultaneously ("2004 Indian Ocean earthquake," 2019). This effort assisted communities to regroup, rebuild, and secure their infrastructure, economy, housing, and school development. During those unbearable, heartbreaking, and seemingly inescapable moments in the survivors' lives, a helping hand, a lending ear, and the sympathetic and empathetic nature of people who contributed to this relief project became the tangible manifestation of a compassionate heart. Question, can you say that you are surrounded by people who have compassionate hearts? Reflect on that question for a moment. A compassionate-hearted person, whether it be a family member, friend, coworker, etc., will always be there to help you to defeat the challenge, as opposed to leaving you to defend for yourself. As a result, your compassionate-hearted relationships - friends, family members included - will without hesitation undergird you during a challenge, uplifting you to stay above the challenge and uncover any brokenness, insecurities, or weaknesses that can weigh you down and prevent you from going through the challenge if not dealt with accordingly.

Let's conclude this chapter by highlighting the four types of people every woman (men included) should embrace in their life in the good times as well as the not so good times.

Friend # 1: A Friend That Makes You Laugh.

It is a must have to have at least one friend that you depend on to make you laugh. As a I indicated in the chapter, when an individual employs laughter, it immediately intervenes by becoming the sword that pierces through the thickness of the problem so that an individual can get a glimpse of sunlight, causing her to press through the situation so that she can arise to a new level of strength with a greater capacity to do what she was called to do in life. I recall a situation in my life when I was so consumed about a situation to the point that mental clarity and emotional stability was becoming a struggle to maintain. How many of you can relate? As I was staring out of my kitchen window, I received a call from my close friend/cousin, Elbert. He had me laughing so hard that I was in tears. That was his mission for that day. His call was unexpected, but the timing was impeccable. At that moment, my mind and emotions disconnected from the situation and began to fellowship with laughter, receiving the dose of medicine needed to strengthen and encourage me to move forward. I have found that when you can laugh, you are giving your mind and emotions a break to regroup for the journey ahead.

Friend # 2: A Good Listener.

You will find that not everyone will fit the job description of a good listener, nor will their resume qualify them as being a potential candidate because they never took the time to cultivate their listening skills. Being a good listener is a craft and art that must be perfected over time as one fully understands and respects the nuances between hearing and listening. The individual who occupies this role of a listener in your life gives you the platform to speak freely and only interjects as needed. Most importantly, this individual shows no signs of being judgmental as you share the brokenness, pain, insecurities, hurts, disappointments, and hidden regrets that have come out of hibernation during your personal tsunami experience.

Friend # 3: The Straight Shooter.

A friend that serves in the capacity of a straight shooter will tell you just like it is. There is no beating around the bush, no sugar coating, no watering down the lemonade, but this individual (or individuals) keeps you on the straight and narrow path as he or she tells you what you need to hear rather than what you want to hear. Straight shooters, whether it be your father, aunt, best friend, coworker, husband, boyfriend, mother, or pastor, provide their insightful overview or "spin" on the matter at hand so that you can do the following: 1) determine if you handled the situation correctly, and 2) see things from a different angle or perspective in order to determine how you could have addressed things differently. During this process, there is another level of maturity that is obtainable if you keep yourself open to receive what the straight shooter is trying to convey to you, knowing that he or she has your best interest at heart. Absorbing what is essential for you to learn from the experience, the challenge will not only allow you to navigate through the storms of life but strengthen you for the next challenge of life.

Friend #4: The Dreams and Goals Supporter.

Some of the most moving inspirational speeches, the most heartfelt love ballads, bestselling books, etc., were birthed from a tsunami experience. Just because you are going through does not mean that you must stop creating, dreaming, inspiring others, or giving of self. Your dreams, inventiveness, and inspirational words are patiently waiting for you to activate the potential on the inside so that your dream or creativity can become tangible and purposeful not only in your life but the lives of others. The time spent dwelling on the situation can be redirected towards sharing and setting goals with a friend or family member who can visualize you on the other side of the storm possessing the physical manifestation of your dream.

Reflection Questions

1. When you encounter a challenge, what is your first response?

Reflection Questions

2. Finish this statement: I refuse to allow a
   challenge to make . . .

Chapter 12

IN THE MIDST OF A STORM

Words of Substance

What word describes you after each challenge you experienced in life - bold, brave, resilient, strong, overcomer, blessed, survivor, determined? There should always be a word(s) that defines your victorious moment after each challenge. These descriptive words are not just any ordinary words that have been randomly selected from the dictionary, but rather words which came to life, rose to the occasion in the midst of pain, hurt, discomfort, pressure, struggle, anguish, disbelief, disappointments, mental torment, and loneliness. You see, words that are life-driven will encourage you, undergird you, protect you, redirect you, and refine you as you maintain mental clarity and emotional stability needed to go through and come out of the storm. You will discover that words carry an enormous amount of weight. Words spoken become a Picasso who paints a portrait on the canvas of your imagination, creating a focal point which assists you in keeping your mind set above the challenge, rather than being absorbed with what is right in front of you. The relevance of reprogramming your mind with words full of life is that it disrupts thoughts that try to distract you from doing what needs to be done at that moment. After presenting at a conference in Galveston, Texas, I had the opportunity to correspond with a young lady who told me that she periodically suffered from anxiety attacks, which hindered her from completing her daily tasks. I instructed her to verbally employ (speak out loud) the word "peace" every time she felt anxious.

See, I knew once she started saying the word "peace" she would see herself at peace; and when she saw herself at peace, then her emotions and feelings would line up with the thought. Her actions (i.e., completing daily tasks, relaxing, being at ease, etc.) would then reflect the word peace; therefore, the thoughts of being anxious, which were aiming towards averting her from doing what she needed to do, would be disrupted.

A Letter of Encouragement. I have learned from the ups and downs of life that during the ins and outs of adversities, you cannot depend on people to encourage you, but you have to learn how to encourage yourself. People - the Aunt Margaret's, coworkers, that neighborhood lady who bakes those delicious, mouth-watering chocolate chip macadamia nut cookies on the holidays - they mean well, but they are not always accessible to give you the encouragement you need at the time you need it. There are nuances for encouragement. A hug, a gentle touch, a smile, uplifting words, and one's demeanor can become like an IV which infuses strength, confirmation through one's mental and emotional veins.

So, what do you when there are moments when your mind, emotions, and even your physically body are trying to persuade you to wave white flags as a sign of surrendering to the fierce storms in your life? My suggestion is not to give up. As long as you can get a glimpse of yourself on the other side of the storm, the challenge you are currently facing is conquerable. As a therapist, during the therapeutic process I would have my clients, especially clients who were experiencing depression, to write a letter of encouragement. The content contained in this written assignment consisted of the following: 1) a personalized greeting (i.e., Dear Jane), 2) recognition of past and present accomplishments, 3) encouraging words that will support or validate in addition to reprogramming the mind, redirecting the emotions and reconstructing the person's inner image, and 4) a closing ending with "Your truly" and their signatures. The client or clients would then insert the letter in an envelope, place a stamp on it, and mail it to be delivered to my office and discussed during the next session. This technique is quite refreshing and healing to one's body, mind, and soul. Beautiful ladies, I strongly recommend that you write an encouragement letter to yourself during those times when you feel like you are being bullied by the challenge you are facing in life. Pick up a pen and become that ready writer who provides words that not only uplift your spirit but reassure you that this too will pass. When no one is accessible to provide you with words of encouragement, learn how to encourage yourself.

I Wish You Well

Often as women, men included, we mentally engage in a private "woe is me" pity party. This exclusive party is where we convince ourselves that we are the only one going through a storm. Not realizing that there is nothing new under the sun, we don't acknowledge that many are experiencing or have experienced the same thing we are currently facing in life.

As I indicated earlier, a challenge can cause you to be self-centered, demanding your thoughts, words, and actions while prolonging its visit in your life. In other words, a challenge thrives off you continuously acknowledging its existence by you giving it your undivided attention. However, the secret behind overcoming a challenge is knowing how to rise above the storm. Eagles have a navigational capability that causes them to master the skill of riding above storms. Eagles avail themselves of the wind of the storm to tower in a matter of seconds, reserving their own energy.

Now, just like eagles have mastered riding above the storm to reserve their energy during the storm, you must tower over the fear, worry, stress, anxiety, and depression . . . that mercilessly tries to drain your energy so that you become encapsulated in the storm. "I Wish You Well," your first response (Ch. 11), "I refuse" statement (Ch. 11), "Letter of encouragement," and "Words of substance" elevate you above the storms so that you can avoid being submerged and shuffled around.

So, what does "I wish you well" entail? I'm glad you asked. It is an unselfish act of kindness that pays profitable dividends to one's emotional, mental, and physical health. I will never forget the time my husband and I had to present at a professional development training in Texas. When I walked in the building, there were 500 participants laughing while engaging in conversation as they were eating lunch. You would think that my eyes would have been drawn to the seemingly delectable catered meal, but my attention was being drawn to the silver, little buckets and the stickies that were placed in front of each participant. I asked the director of the organization, "What was the purpose behind the buckets and stickies?" She indicated that the participants had the opportunity of writing "I wish you well" notes to any or everyone present during the in-service training. Each personalized note either contained words of encouragement to support an individual during challenging times or to recognize his or her accomplishments. I witnessed a lot of hugs, tears, and laughter that day as love became the voice which echoed "I Wish You Well" to all those who were present. From that day forward, I was compelled to incorporate this heartfelt activity into our customized mental health series.

So, how does "I Wish You Well" benefit us as women (and men) during those uncomfortable, unbearable, and teachable moments in our lives? I'm glad you asked! What I have extracted from the nature of this simple but powerful sacrificial act is the following:

1. **It takes the focus off you and places it on someone else who is in need of his or her spirits being uplifted. This sacrificial act repositions you from self-centeredness to people-centeredness, and as a result, brings relief to the mind and emotions as they escape from being barricaded within the internal pressures of the challenge at hand;**

2. **It gives you the opportunity to sow seeds. Sowing seeds such as laughter, encouragement, monetary means, time, a helping hand, food,**

etc., into the lives of others causes you to reap a bountiful harvest of both mental and emotional gratification; and

3. It heightens your ability to be sensitive or discern those who are in need of a breath of fresh air as they maneuver through the transitions of life. The genuineness of your contribution, either through words or deeds, becomes an unexpected but timely encouragement and/or confirmation needed to bolster one's mental clarity and emotional stability. "I wish you well" has its own boomerang effect, which returns to the originator peace, a sense of accomplishment, satisfaction, gratification, encouragement, and even strength that readily begins to realign the mind and emotions as you courageously overcome the challenge at hand. "I Wish You Well," strong and beautiful ladies, as you diligently wear your many hats, even in the midst of a storm.

Reflection Questions

1. What word describes you after each challenge you experienced in life?

Reflection Questions

2. Briefly, if you wrote a letter of encouragement to yourself, what would you say?

Chapter 13

WORDS OF WISDOM
WHILE ON THE JOURNEY

There is so much that I want to impart into your lives, but wisdom would have it that I allow you to extract the nutrients/ substance contained in each chapter of this book and apply them accordingly as you deposit life back into your mind and emotions. Hopefully, each chapter of this book is filled with pages where the corner of the pages are either bent or highlighted with a bright yellow marker of what you found to be relevant and helpful to interject in your life for your personal growth and development. I am sure the many hats you wear may require a lot from you but is vital for you to guard and nurture your internal reality, your heart, and your soul so that there will always be a continuous outpouring of wisdom available to support you as you fulfill your assignments in life.

As we depart and go down our individual paths in life, I would like to supply you with 60 days of words of wisdom that will feed you during your journey. Our paths will cross again within the pages of another book, but until then, wear the new version with style for you are a Masterpiece!

CHALLENGE

Challenge your adversities in life by refusing to allow your mind, emotions, actions, and words confirm their existence.

PATTERN

Your pattern of thinking has a significant impact on the way you respond to life. How you respond to life will determine if you are mastering life or if life is mastering you.

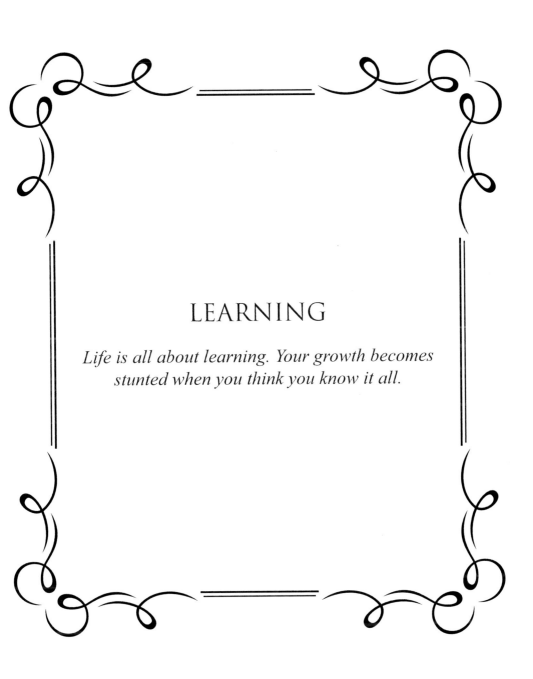

LEARNING

Life is all about learning. Your growth becomes stunted when you think you know it all.

TRUE FRIEND

A true friend does not tell you what you want to hear but rather what you need to hear so you can examine yourself, make the adjustments, and move on.

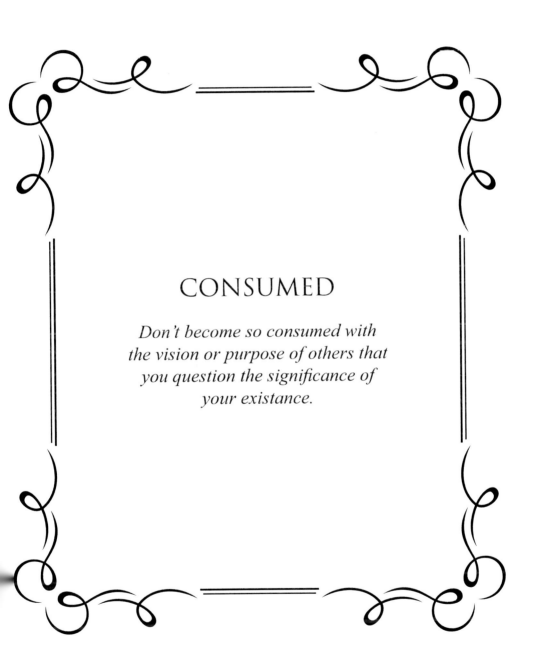

CONSUMED

Don't become so consumed with the vision or purpose of others that you question the significance of your existance.

GIVE

Never get to the point that you cannot compliment, encourage and even support those around you because the essence of your purpose in life is to GIVE.

STAY IN YOUR LANE

*People change, situations change, but
what remains the same is your purpose
in life. Stay in your lane, keep your peace
and do what you were assigned to do!*

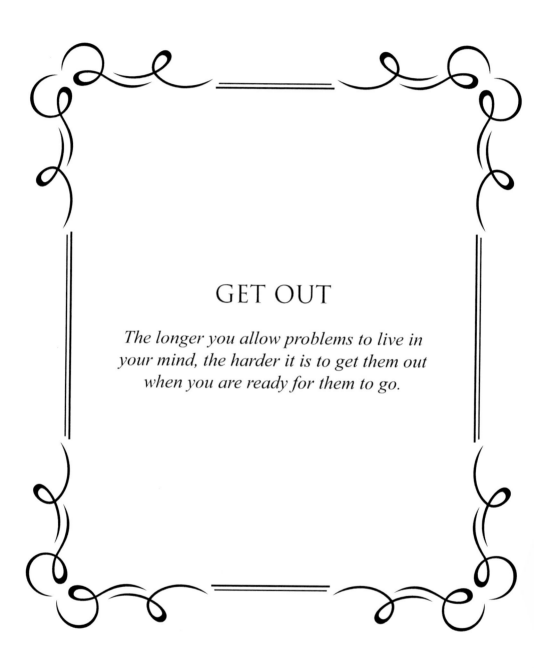

GET OUT

The longer you allow problems to live in your mind, the harder it is to get them out when you are ready for them to go.

GIVE

Never get to the point that you cannot compliment, encourage and even support those around you, because the essence of your purpose in life is to GIVE.

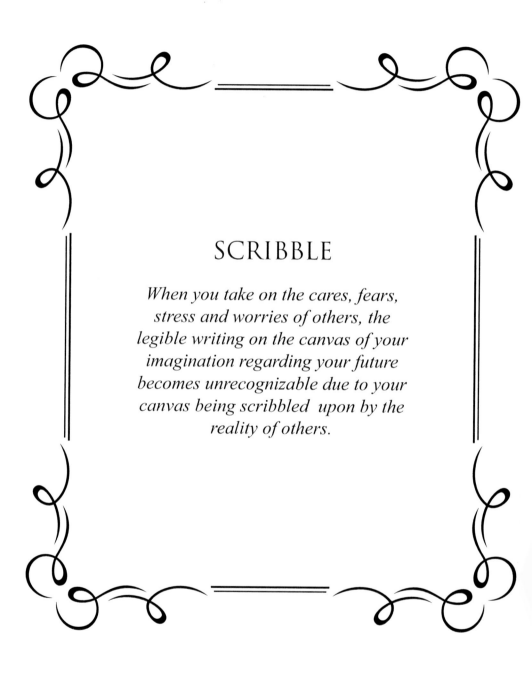

SCRIBBLE

When you take on the cares, fears, stress and worries of others, the legible writing on the canvas of your imagination regarding your future becomes unrecognizable due to your canvas being scribbled upon by the reality of others.

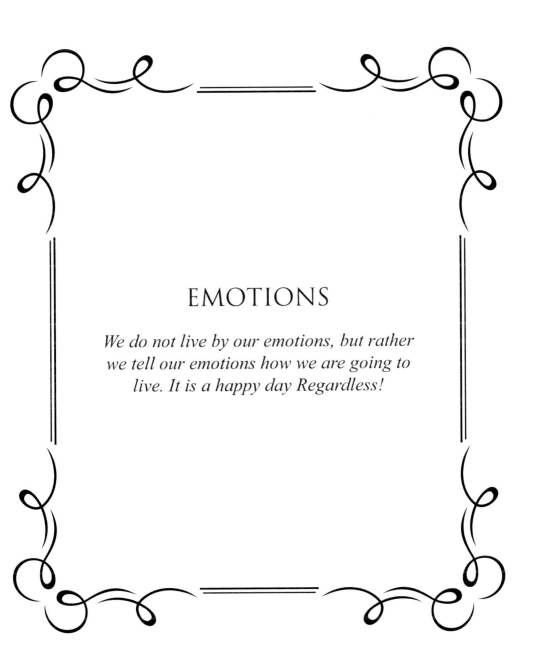

EMOTIONS

We do not live by our emotions, but rather we tell our emotions how we are going to live. It is a happy day Regardless!

CALM

Set your emotional radio dial
on CALM FM and keep it there.
Regardless of the distractions that may
come your way, do not touch that dial!
It is a happy day, regardless!

KEEP IT MOVING

Stop always thinking you have done something wrong when people act like they do not want to be bothered. Don't take it personally. Let them have their space, keep your mind on things that are of a good report, and keep it moving.

STAY IN YOUR LANE

People change, situations change, but what remains the same is your purpose in life. Stay in your lane, keep your peace and do what you were assigned to do!

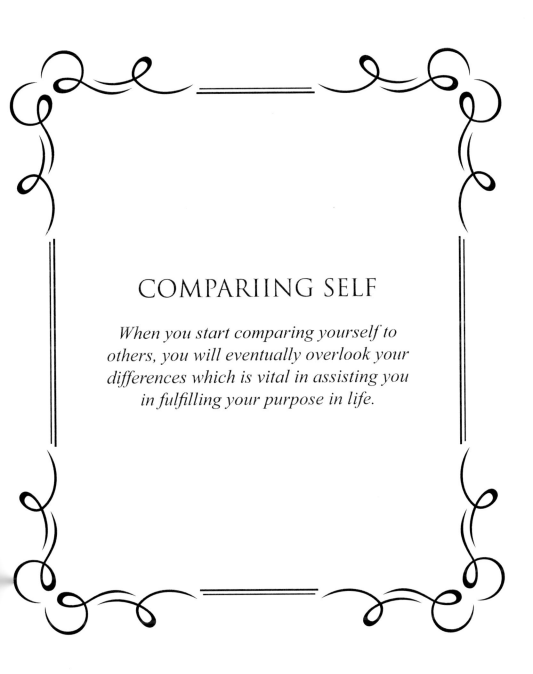

COMPARIING SELF

When you start comparing yourself to others, you will eventually overlook your differences which is vital in assisting you in fulfilling your purpose in life.

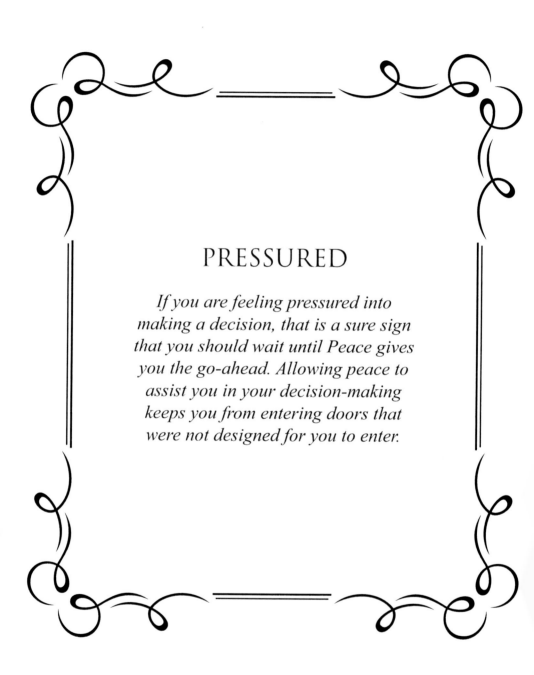

PRESSURED

If you are feeling pressured into making a decision, that is a sure sign that you should wait until Peace gives you the go-ahead. Allowing peace to assist you in your decision-making keeps you from entering doors that were not designed for you to enter.

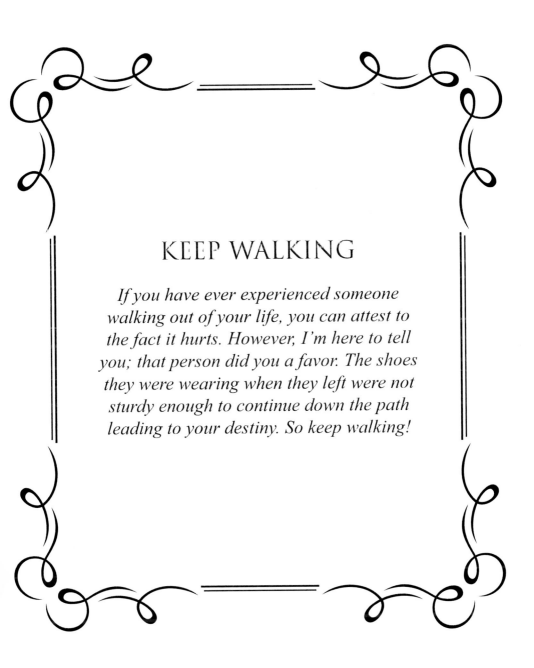

KEEP WALKING

If you have ever experienced someone walking out of your life, you can attest to the fact it hurts. However, I'm here to tell you; that person did you a favor. The shoes they were wearing when they left were not sturdy enough to continue down the path leading to your destiny. So keep walking!

PLATFORM

The best platform you could ever have in life is being a positive example to those around you.

ENTERTAIN

If you continue to entertain the fears of others, you will eventually find yourself part of the show. Never, Never, Never allow fears of someone else to become your reality.

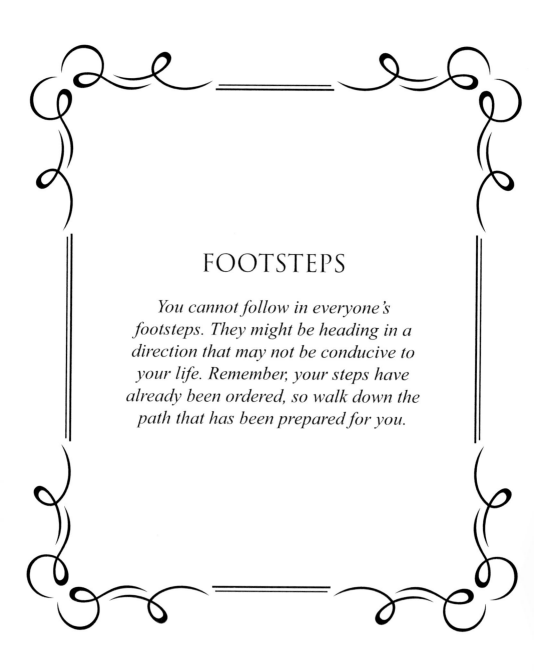

FOOTSTEPS

You cannot follow in everyone's footsteps. They might be heading in a direction that may not be conducive to your life. Remember, your steps have already been ordered, so walk down the path that has been prepared for you.

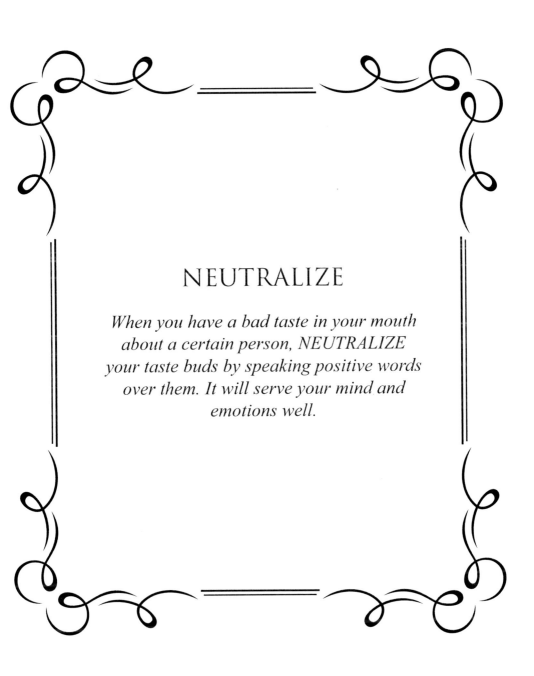

NEUTRALIZE

When you have a bad taste in your mouth about a certain person, NEUTRALIZE your taste buds by speaking positive words over them. It will serve your mind and emotions well.

FORGIVE YOURSELF

Forgive yourself, move on, and do what you were called to do in life. You past is your past, and you should never allow it to share the stage with your destiny.

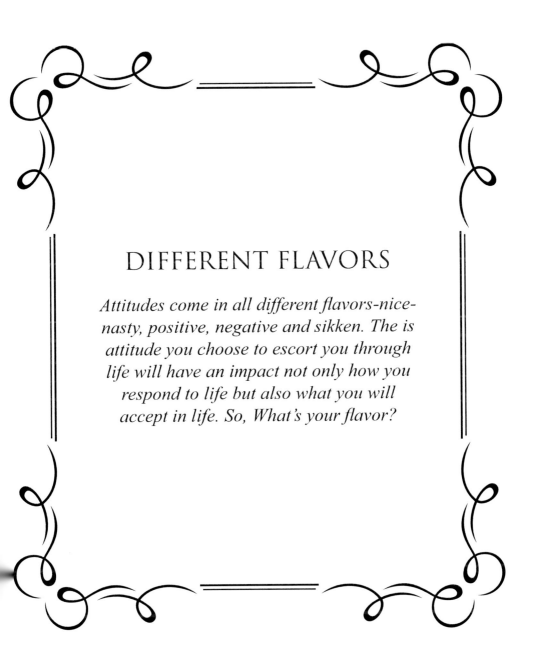

DIFFERENT FLAVORS

Attitudes come in all different flavors-nice-nasty, positive, negative and sikken. The is attitude you choose to escort you through life will have an impact not only how you respond to life but also what you will accept in life. So, What's your flavor?

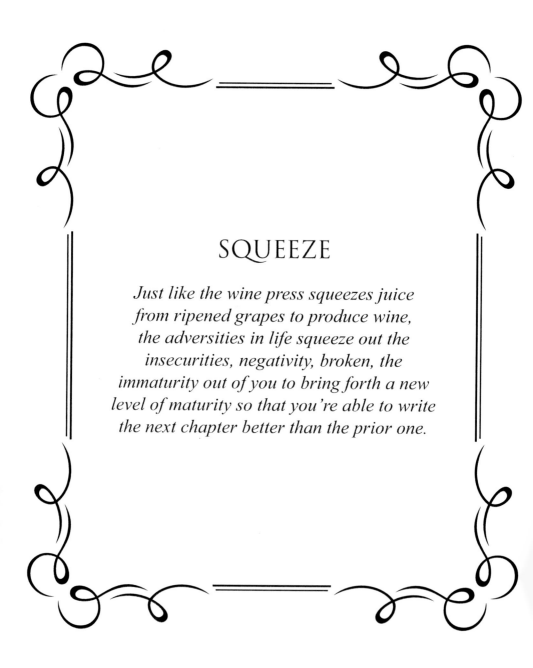

SQUEEZE

*Just like the wine press squeezes juice
from ripened grapes to produce wine,
the adversities in life squeeze out the
insecurities, negativity, broken, the
immaturity out of you to bring forth a new
level of maturity so that you're able to write
the next chapter better than the prior one.*

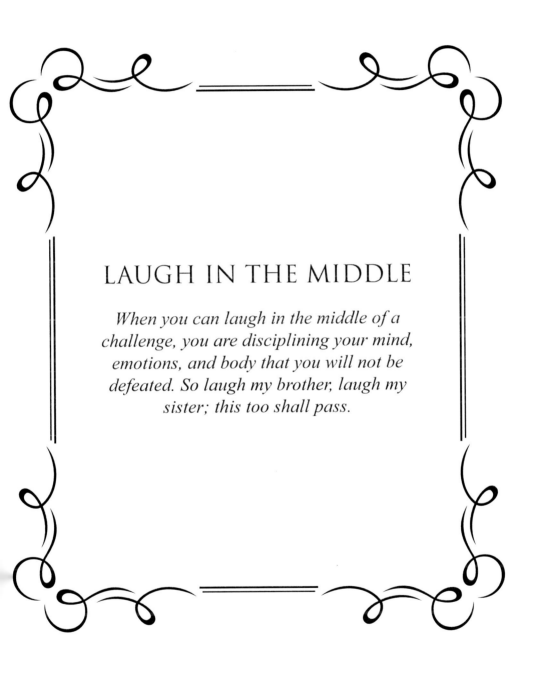

LAUGH IN THE MIDDLE

When you can laugh in the middle of a challenge, you are disciplining your mind, emotions, and body that you will not be defeated. So laugh my brother, laugh my sister; this too shall pass.

PAIRING

Stop "PAIRING" your mind with people, places and things that are incompatible with your purpose in life. DISCONNECT!!!

GRATEFUL MOMENTS

*When was it last time you had a
"Grateful" moment? You will find during
those moments that you have more to be
grateful for rather than complain about.
YOU ARE A MASTERPIECE!*

WAITING

Your dream is waiting for you to mature so that you can carry it safely without being concerned about it being dropped just because someone says your dream will not come to fruition.

HANDWRITING

Your character is like your handwriting.
The actions you display can be read
without you ever saying a word.

MOVING FORWARD

When you keep moving forward, life pushes your past further away. Bringing your past life into your future hinders you from seizing those moments that carry the opportunities that were custom-made just for you!

THE SHOW

If you continue to entertain the fears of others, you will eventually find yourself part of the show. Never allow someone's fear to become your reality.

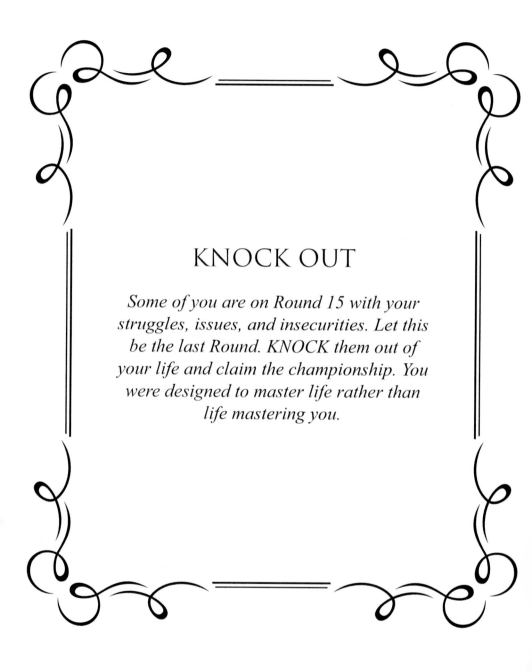

KNOCK OUT

Some of you are on Round 15 with your struggles, issues, and insecurities. Let this be the last Round. KNOCK them out of your life and claim the championship. You were designed to master life rather than life mastering you.

ILLEGAL

S- Stress is a THIEF and will ROB you of your:
T- Time
R- Rest
E- Energy
S- Soundness of mind
S- Sensitivity towards others

Stress can only do what YOU allow it to do.

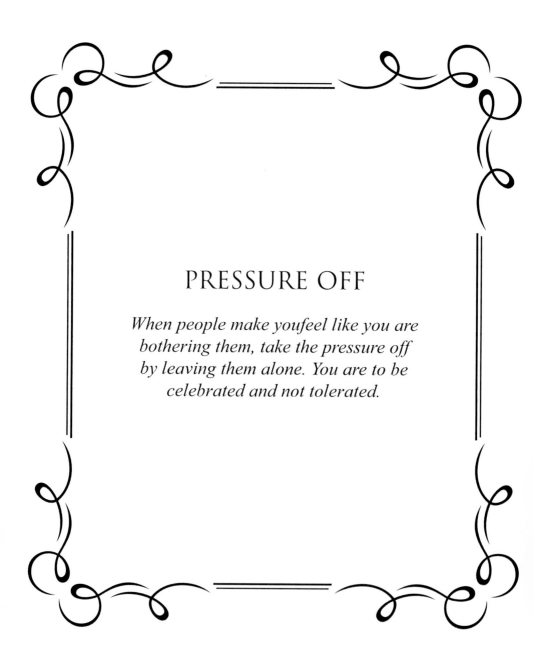

PRESSURE OFF

When people make you feel like you are bothering them, take the pressure off by leaving them alone. You are to be celebrated and not tolerated.

REFUSE

Refuse to drown in depression, fear, stress, loneliness, what if's, pity, complaining, rejection, anxiety, worry, shame, guilt; get in the boat with PEACE, turn the outboard motor on, and keep on moving. You were not designed to drown, but to stay afloat.

KNOWING

Knowing when to speak and when to be silent is not a skill, but wisdom.

MOVE

Stop dwelling on your past. Renovate your mind so that you can move to where your future resides.

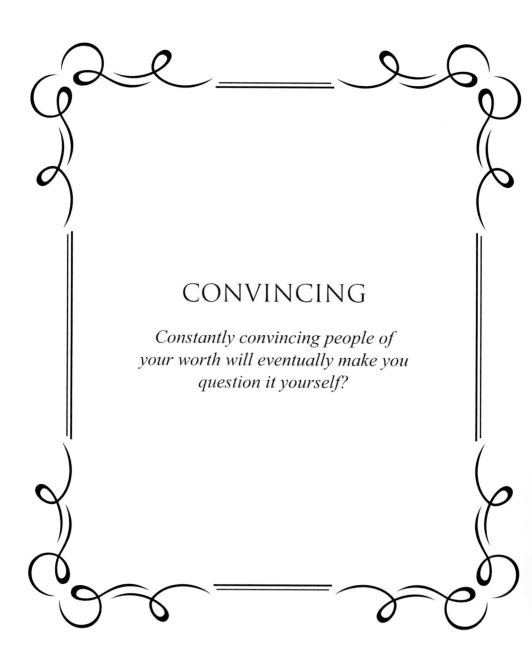

CONVINCING

Constantly convincing people of your worth will eventually make you question it yourself?

WAITING

Your dream is waiting for you to mature so that you can carry it safely without being concerned about it being dropped just because someone says your dream will not come to fruition.

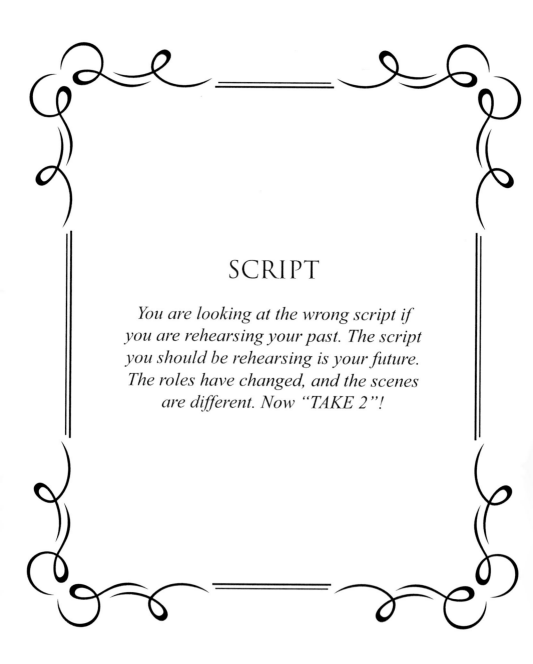

SCRIPT

You are looking at the wrong script if you are rehearsing your past. The script you should be rehearsing is your future. The roles have changed, and the scenes are different. Now "TAKE 2"!

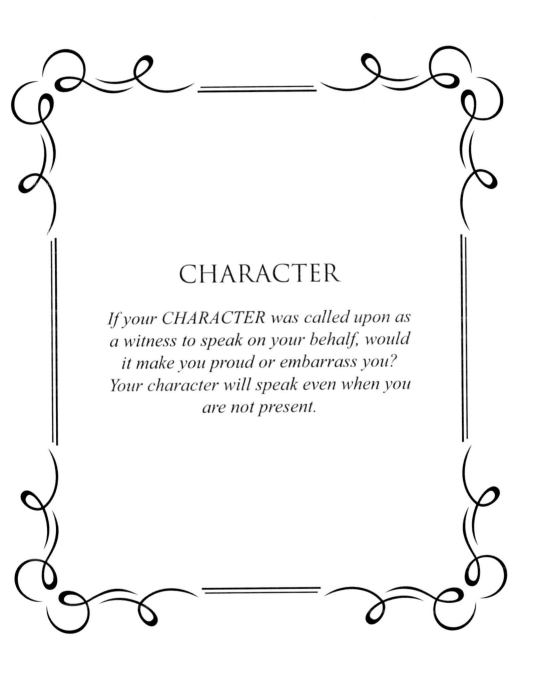

CHARACTER

If your CHARACTER was called upon as a witness to speak on your behalf, would it make you proud or embarrass you? Your character will speak even when you are not present.

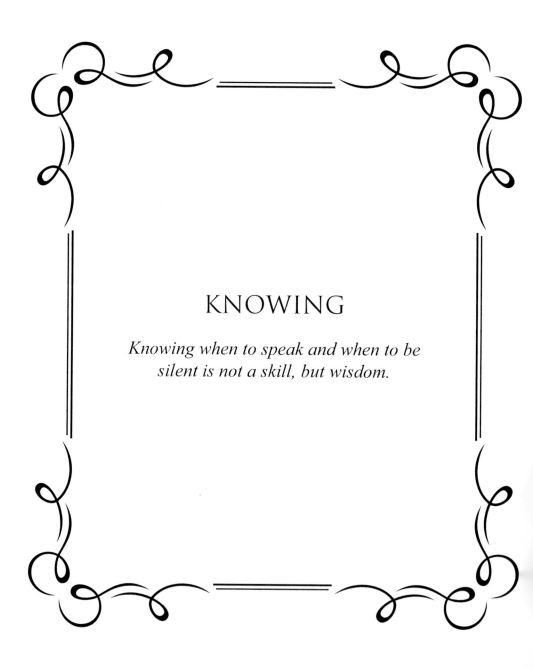

KNOWING

Knowing when to speak and when to be silent is not a skill, but wisdom.

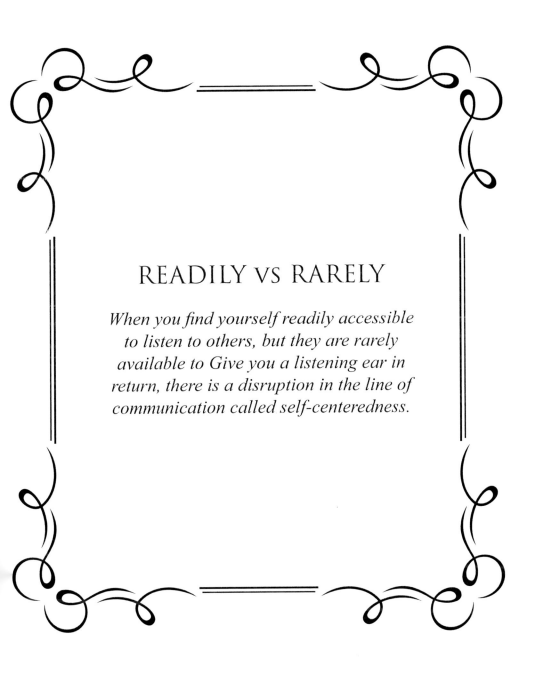

READILY vs RARELY

*When you find yourself readily accessible
to listen to others, but they are rarely
available to Give you a listening ear in
return, there is a disruption in the line of
communication called self-centeredness.*

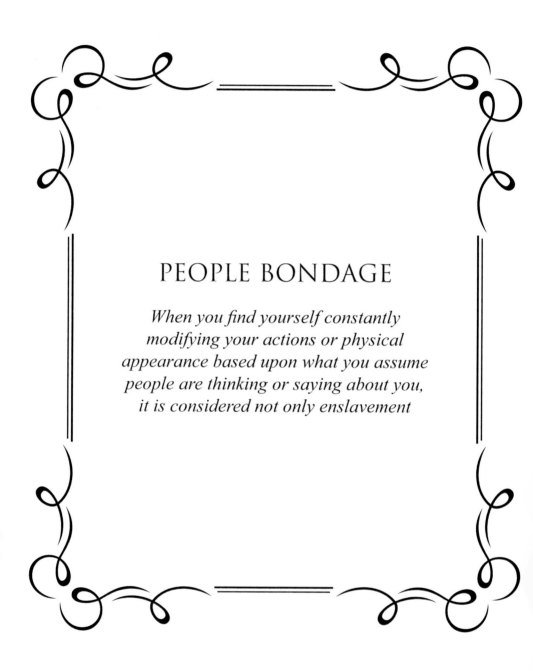

PEOPLE BONDAGE

*When you find yourself constantly
modifying your actions or physical
appearance based upon what you assume
people are thinking or saying about you,
it is considered not only enslavement*

RECOGNIZE AND EMBRACE

*Some people are more comfortable displaying
average because they feel unworthy of wearing
opulence. Recognize and Embrace the Royalty
in you, and wear it well.*

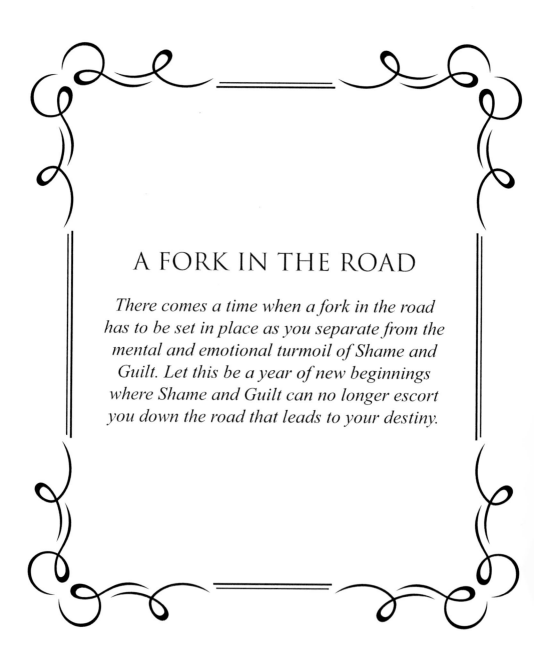

A FORK IN THE ROAD

*There comes a time when a fork in the road
has to be set in place as you separate from the
mental and emotional turmoil of Shame and
Guilt. Let this be a year of new beginnings
where Shame and Guilt can no longer escort
you down the road that leads to your destiny.*

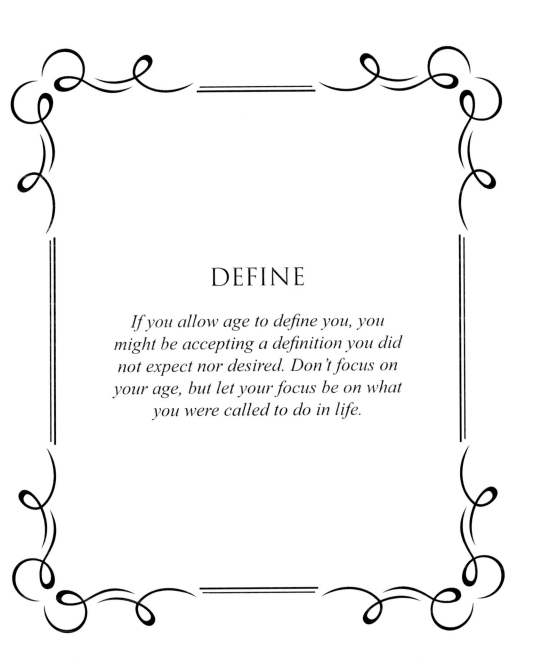

DEFINE

If you allow age to define you, you might be accepting a definition you did not expect nor desired. Don't focus on your age, but let your focus be on what you were called to do in life.

SEASON

Your season for imparting into the lives of others may have ended, but your love for them will never change. Sometimes you just have to release people and pass the baton over to life to reinforce what you were trying to say.

STAND UP

Refuse to sit in your situation and be absorbed with what is in front of you. STAND UP and see all that is in store for you on the other side. If you employ the canvas of your imagination, you will realize you are never stuck!

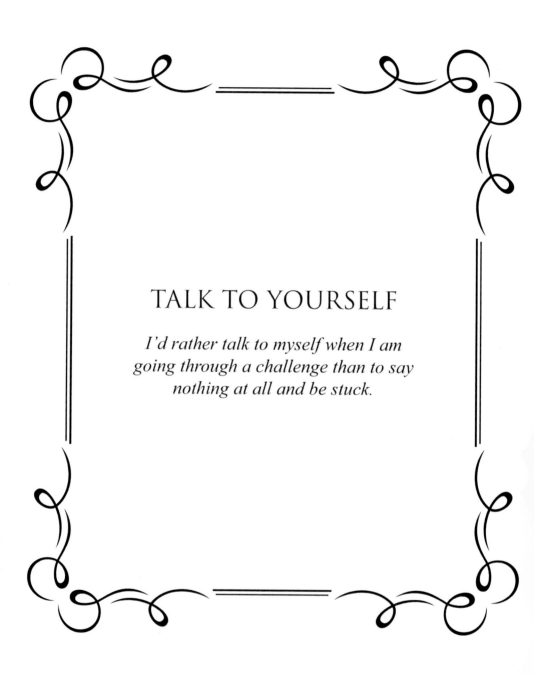

TALK TO YOURSELF

I'd rather talk to myself when I am going through a challenge than to say nothing at all and be stuck.

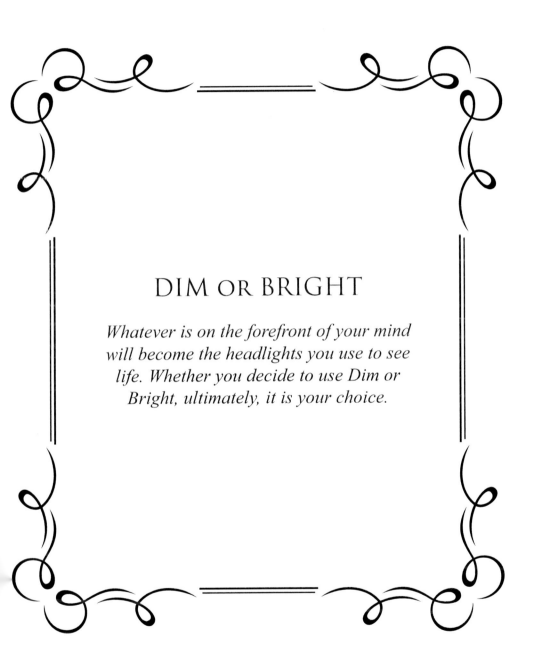

DIM OR BRIGHT

Whatever is on the forefront of your mind will become the headlights you use to see life. Whether you decide to use Dim or Bright, ultimately, it is your choice.

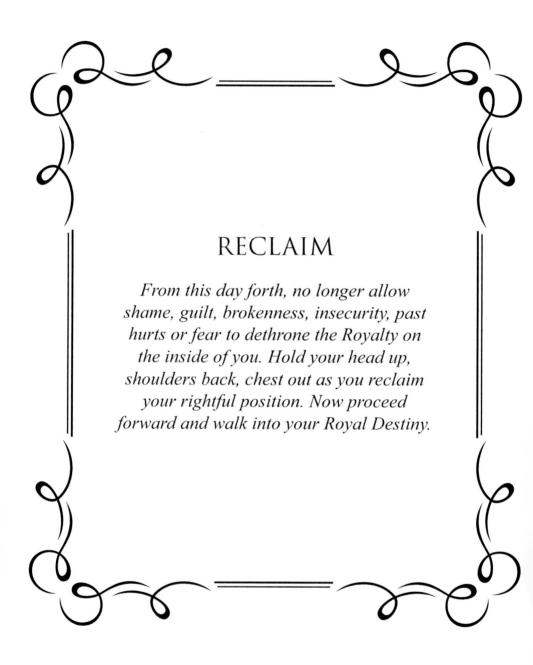

RECLAIM

From this day forth, no longer allow shame, guilt, brokenness, insecurity, past hurts or fear to dethrone the Royalty on the inside of you. Hold your head up, shoulders back, chest out as you reclaim your rightful position. Now proceed forward and walk into your Royal Destiny.

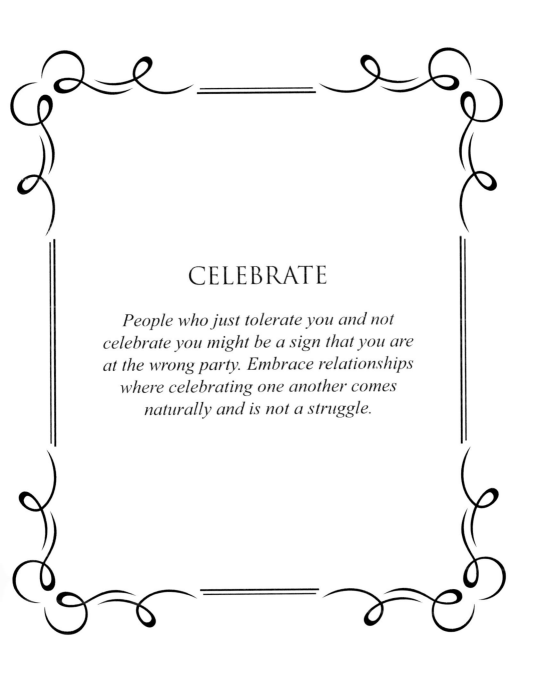

CELEBRATE

People who just tolerate you and not celebrate you might be a sign that you are at the wrong party. Embrace relationships where celebrating one another comes naturally and is not a struggle.

THE ENTIRE SET

Allowing people to use you only as a Sounding Board but ignoring your words of wisdom gives them permission to pick and choose rather than getting the entire set. My advice, guard your heart and refuse to allow people's drama to become a box office hit in your mind.

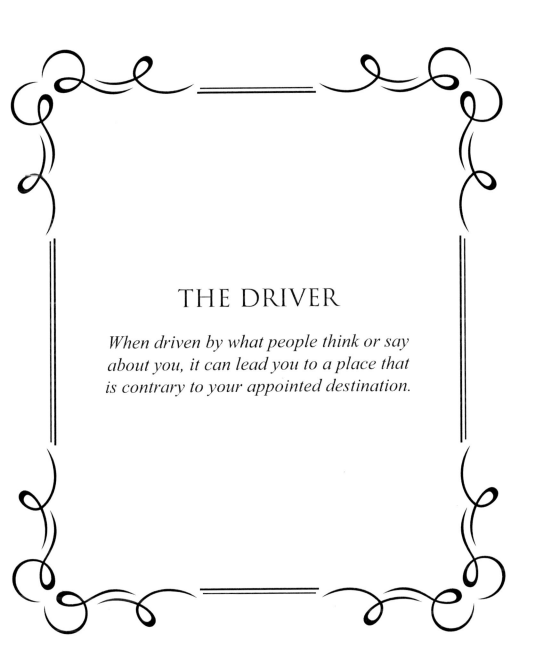

THE DRIVER

When driven by what people think or say about you, it can lead you to a place that is contrary to your appointed destination.

FULL SAIL AHEAD

*Full Sail Alread! You can only be on the
island of depression, unforgiveness, past
betrayal, hurt, disappointments, negativity
and lingering insecurities for so long until
it is time for you to gather your emotions
and mind; get in the boat, and push off.*

*Never look back nor return to the place
which has held you captive. Enough is
enough! FULL SAIL AHEAD!*

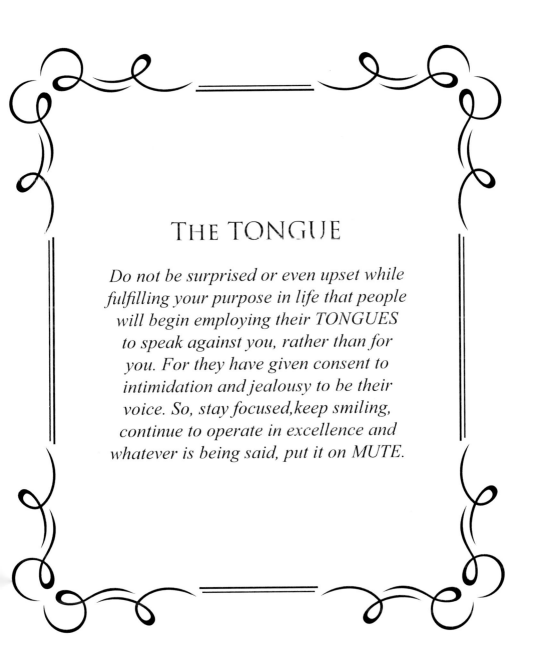

THE TONGUE

Do not be surprised or even upset while fulfilling your purpose in life that people will begin employing their TONGUES to speak against you, rather than for you. For they have given consent to intimidation and jealousy to be their voice. So, stay focused,keep smiling, continue to operate in excellence and whatever is being said, put it on MUTE.

SHIFTS

*Why do we experience shifts in our lives?
Shifts are life experiences that challenge
you and I to leave a place of familiarity and
enter a place of unfamiliarity. It Is during
those unfamiliar moments that we have
"growth spurts," every time we step out on
faith and embrace the Importance of being
teachable. As a result of these "growth
spurts," you and I are now qualified to write
the next chapter based on experience and
not just hear say only.*

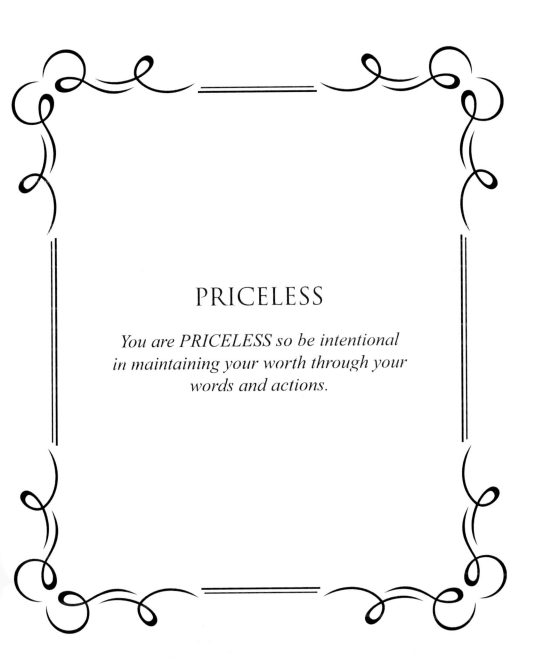

PRICELESS

*You are PRICELESS so be intentional
in maintaining your worth through your
words and actions.*

WILDERNESS

Complaining creates a mental wilderness that will take you deeper than you want to go and keep you longer than you want to be kept. When tempted to complain, be intentional in giving thanks.

References

Definition of toxic. (2022). *Merriam-Webster Dictionary*, https://www.merriam-webster.com/dictionary/toxic

Ferber, D. (2007, January 30). The health benefits of laughter. *Women's Health*. https://www.womenshealthmag.com/life/a19968254/live-laugh-love/

Leaf, C. (2009). Who switched off my brain? Controlling toxic thoughts and emotions. Thomas Nelson, Inc.

Trimm, C. (2020). *Goodbye, yesterday!: Activating the 12 laws of boundary-defying faith*. Charisma House.

2004 Indian Ocean earthquake and tsunami. (2022). *Wikipedia*. https://en.wikipedia.org/w/index.php?title=2004_

2004 Indian Ocean earthquake and tsunami: Facts, FAQs, and how to help. (2019, December 26). *World Vision*. https://www.worldvision.org/disaster-relief-news-stories/2004-indian-ocean-earthquake-tsunami-facts

Why you should nap more. (2020, June 13). *WebMD*. https://www.webmd.com/a-to-z-guides/ss/slideshow-health-benefits-of-napping

About the Author

Sheryl Brown is a licensed minister and motivational speaker. She travels extensively empowering women to master life rather than life mastering them. Sheryl holds a Bachelors of Science degree in Biology, Masters in Public Administration, and a Masters of Science in Counseling Psychology-Marriage and Family Therapy. She is a licensed marriage family therapist who specializes in family and children therapy. In addition, she is a Certified Child Development Intervention Specialist.

Sheryl is the author of *Push: How to Birth Your Dreams into Reality*, *What All Children Want: Structure*, and *Productive Little Citizens: Developing an Emotionally Supportive Community*.